4703

PROPERTY OF
SHAARE SHAMAYIM-BETH JUDAH LIBRARY
9768 VERREE ROAD
PHILADELPHIA, PA 19115-1996

It All
Begins
with a Date

Shaare Shamayim - Beth Judah

In Memory of

Joseph Rubin

Dedicated By

Jerry & Sherry Hershfield

It All Begins with a Date

Jewish Concerns about Intermarriage

ALAN SILVERSTEIN

A Project of
The Leadership Council of Conservative Judaism

4703

JASON ARONSON INC.
Northvale, New Jersey
London

This book was set in 11 point Palacio by AeroType, Inc. in Amherst, New Hampshire.

Copyright © 1995 Alan Silverstein

10 9 8 7 6 5 4 3 2

All rights reserved. Printed in the United States of America. No part of this book may be used or reproduced in any manner whatsoever without written permission from Jason Aronson Inc. except in the case of brief quotations in reviews for inclusion in a magazine, newspaper, or broadcast.

Library of Congress Cataloging-in-Publication Data

Silverstein, Alan.
    It all begins with a date : Jewish concerns about intermarriage /
by Alan Silverstein
        p.   cm.
    Includes bibliographical references and index.
    ISBN 1-56821-542-8
    1. Interfaith marriage–United States. 2. Jews–United States–
Identity. 3. Marriage–Religious aspects–Judaism. 4. Jewish
families–Religious life–United States. 5. Conservative Judaism–
United States.   I. Title
HQ1031.S48 1995
306.84'3--dc20   95-9255
                                                              CIP

Manufactured in the United States of America. Jason Aronson Inc. offers books and cassettes. For information and catalog write to Jason Aronson Inc., 230 Livingston Street, Northvale, New Jersey 07647.

For my in-laws

Cili and Sol Neufeld

Contents

Foreword: Mobilizing Conservative Judaism's Institutions—
Promoting Marriage within the Faith   *Jerome Epstein*   xvii

Acknowledgments   xxi

Introduction   xxiii

1 Grounds for Concern: Jewish Views of Intermarriage   1

   1. Rabbi, throughout my years in Hebrew school and Jewish
     youth groups, no one ever showed me where Jewish
     sacred texts oppose intermarriage. From my perspective,
     it seems as though such stubbornness is simply parental
     narrow-mindedness and that it has no basis in Jewish
     religion.   4

   2. Okay, Rabbi, perhaps individual verses in the Bible and
     Jewish law prohibited interfaith marriage; however,
     many of the great ancient Jewish leaders such as Moses
     and Joseph clearly disregarded these strictures.   7

   3. Rabbi, perhaps Jewish sources oppose intermarriage and
     postulate that an intermarrying Jew and his/her descen-
     dants will be lost to Judaism, but can't I resolve this
     problem by marrying a non-Jewish person and having
     that individual convert to Judaism?   8

4. If my non-Jewish spouse does not convert to Judaism, can't I still perpetuate Judaism by raising my children as Jews? 9

5. Why not raise my future offspring without any religion at all? 11

6. Why not raise the children in both Judaism and Christianity? 12

7. Why not expose sons and daughters to both Judaism and Christianity during childhood and let them make their own choice later in life? 15

8. Regardless of these considerations, can't I have a fine marital relationship anyway? 17

9. Well, at least one thing is for certain. Even if I intermarry and my spouse does not convert, and my children are not certain to be Jews, of course my own Judaism remains assured. 20

10. I can agree that becoming a Catholic or a Protestant means leaving the fold. What about Messianic Judaism as a compromise choice? 21

11. What about Unitarianism as a neutral ground? 22

12. Are there perils in a Jew selecting transcendental meditation as an alternative choice? 25

13. What about turning instead to discipline of the mind such as Scientology? 27

14. What about stepping aside from organized religion and joining a humanistic cause such as Ethical Culture? 30

15. Why doesn't the Jewish community simply solve the problem of disaffiliation by proclaiming non-Jewish spouses and children full participants in local synagogues and in Jewish life in general? 33

16. Rabbi, isn't promoting marriage of one's own kind a view that is incompatible with our commitments to America, democracy, openness, and freedom of choice? 34

17. What difference does it make if—following marriage—I or my new family unit remains Jewish or becomes Christian or some combination of both? Are not all these religions the same, simply teaching you to be a good person? 35

18. Rabbi, why do Christian clergy—ministers and priests—seem less concerned about intermarriage than our Jewish leaders? 38

19. Perhaps all of this is true. But if so, what difference should it make to me? Why be Jewish at all? 40

20. Isn't all of this discussion futile? In our open society, with a reported 50 percent intermarriage rate growing at a rapid pace, is not interfaith marriage inevitable? 42

21. Rabbi, if you are so concerned about the implications of intermarriage, why are you willing to spend so much time working with prospective converts and mixed-marrieds grappling with Judaism? 44

2 Interdating and Intermarriage: A Jewish Parents' Guide 47

1. How would my child's intermarrying pose a risk to Jewish survival? 49

2. My children will never share my point of view. Why bother to engage them in a conversation about inter-dating/intermarriage? It is a waste of time, an exercise in futility.   50

3. Might I be impairing my relationship with my child if he/ she gets angry at my intrusion into his/her dating or marital plans?   53

4. How can I justify my views about Judaism when my children see that I am not observant? Wouldn't I be hypo-critical?   54

5. How can I reconcile concerns about interdating/inter-marriage with my desire for a full involvement in Ameri-can society and an openness to friendships with non-Jews?   58

6. When so many other Jewishly identifying parents take no stand whatsoever against interdating/intermarriage, how can I set myself apart?   60

7. How can I oppose interdating/intermarriage when I ac-cept intermarried members of our extended family?   61

8. What are some of the blessings and joys of being Jewish, having Jewish descendants, being part of the Jewish chain of tradition?   62

9. Beyond dialogue, what actions can I take to diminish the likelihood of my children intermarrying?   63
      High-school Years   63
      The College Experience   65
      After Graduation   66

3 It All Begins with a Date: Parent/Young Adult Dialogues about Interdating **69**

1. Mom/Dad, why are Jews so upset about interdating? Perhaps intermarriage is not acceptable, but dating simply means having a good time, without making a lifelong commitment. Why shouldn't I interdate until the right Jewish person comes along? 72

2. Come on. Isn't saying I won't interdate just another form of racism? 73

3. Aren't the criteria regarding dating different than those related to marriage? 75

4. Mom/Dad, what is the problem of interdating within our circle of non-Jewish friends? After all, we are just like one another in all other ways. Isn't it good to have non-Jewish friends? 77
   Balancing Gentile Friendships with Jewish Dating Patterns 77
   Differences Do Exist 78
   The December Dilemma 79

5. I live in a Jewish community in which there are relatively few Jewish dating partners. Are you suggesting that I not date at all? 80
   Deferring "Fun" 80
   Aggressively Travel to Network with Other Jews 81
   Do Not Panic 81

6. Are all the television and film portrayals of compatible mixed dating and intermarriage off base? 82

7. I have another issue to raise. Jewish prospective dating partners don't seem to have the qualities I seek. 84

8. Why do you (parents/grandparents) interfere in this aspect of my decision-making? This is my life, isn't it? Why can't you be like other parents and leave me alone? Why do you care so much about intermarriage when you are not religious anyway?   89

9. Mom/Dad, aren't you being hypocrites about interdating and intermarriage? After all, you attended my cousin's intermarriage wedding. You accept Aunt Jane and Uncle Ralph's marriage, even though they had interdated and then Jane converted to Judaism. You even accept Aunt Sarah and Uncle John's family. Though John never relinquished his Christianity, their kids are being raised as Jews.   93

4 **Planting Seeds for Jewish Continuity: A Guide for Children Ages 3–6**   **97**

1. Rabbi, how can we answer the question "Why be Jewish?" both for kids and for ourselves?   100

2. Are parents really important role models for the transmission of Judaism to their offspring?   100

3. Does remaining Jewish require that I segregate my children from society, as do some Jewish groups?   102

4. Rabbi, give me an example of this synthesis when the annual December dilemma, Hanukkah vs. Christmas, invades our family's life!   104

5. What shall we say when youngsters ask about intermarriage, about intermarried relatives, about people they know who are interdating, about television shows in

which people are married to persons of different religious backgrounds?   106

6. What other matters must we resolve in our own minds as parents before we can teach our children to have pride as Jews?   109

7. How shall we pursue the goal of making our child into a good Jew, a *mensch*?   110

8. What kinds of hands-on activities add to my child's growing Jewish identity?   113

9. Rabbi, does my child really "need" religion/synagogue after all?   114

10. Rabbi, does Judaism contribute to my child's identity formation and sense of belonging?   118

11. What is the impact of enrolling my child in a program of formal Jewish education? And of informal Jewish settings?   121

12. What is meant by Jewish family education? Is this something that would be important for my family?   123

5 Why Be Jewish? What's the Gain, the Pride, the Joy?   127

Self-Fulfillment via Judaism   130
Heart Jews — Spirituality and Ritual Expression   132
Hand Jews — Assisting Fellow Jews and Social Activism   141
Head Jews — Religious Beliefs and Intellectual Strivings 148

6 Looking Ahead   **161**

Appendix I: Judaism and Christianity Are Different   **167**

   A *Bris* Is Not a Baptism   168
   Bar/Bat Mitzvah Is Not Christian Confirmation   169
   Responses to Death in Judaism and Christianity   171
   Synagogue Is Not Church   172
   Hanukkah Is Not Christmas   173
   Passover Is Not Easter   176

Appendix II: Grandparenting Jewish Children   **179**

  1. Rabbi, since I have not been "religious" up to this point,
     wouldn't it be hypocritical to begin to stress to my chil-
     dren and grandchildren that being Jewish is important to
     me?   180

  2. How powerful are rituals in the transmission process? 181

  3. What do I say if my children accept my newfound Jewish
     lifestyle for my home but refuse to encourage Jewish
     activities for my grandchildren within their own do-
     main?   184

  4. How shall we pursue the goal of making our grandchild
     into a good Jew, a *mensch*?   186

  5. Should I offer to finance the Jewish experiences of my
     grandchildren?   187
       Synagogue Affiliation   188
       Jewish Education   188
       Jewish Informal Activities   188

College and Beyond 189

Conclusion 190

Appendix III: Resource Guide **191**

Publications 191
Additional Recommended Reading 193
Videotapes and Films 196

Appendix IV: Promoting Jewish Continuity: Opportunities Available within Conservative Judaism **197**

Early Childhood 197
Synagogue Schools 197
Solomon Schechter Day Schools 199
Camps Ramah 199
Youth Movements 200
Israel Experience 201
College Life 202
Adult Education 203

Bibliography 205

Index 213

Foreword

Mobilizing Conservative Judaism's Institutions—
Promoting Marriage within the Faith
Jerome Epstein

The Council of Jewish Federations' (CJF) Population Study of 1990 indicated that more than 50 percent of the American Jews who have married since 1985 married non-Jews. Furthermore, the CJF study makes it clear that the Jewish community has lost more members (210,000) through conversion than it has gained in this period (185,000). This data has provided the Jewish community with sufficient information to draw conclusions and construct programs regarding intermarriage. As Dr. Robert Gordis pointed out years ago, "Intermarriage is a royal road to the absorption and disappearance of the [Jewish] people and its tradition." The Conservative movement in American Judaism truly believes that without increased efforts toward promoting marriage within the Jewish faith, the American Jewish community ultimately is in peril.

Statistical support for this prognosis is included in *Children of the Intermarried* by Professor Egon Mayer, a 1983 study of two-faith households. As noted in this book, Dr. Mayer pointed out that 81 percent deemed "unimportant" the simple act of "belonging to the Jewish community." Only 11 percent of the individuals indicated that they would be "very upset" if their sons and daughters "did not regard themselves as Jews." And only 3 percent would "discourage" their offspring "from marrying someone who is not Jewish."

Among many American Jews, the current response to this growing crisis is to throw up our hands and say, "We cannot stop it!" Instead, many urge that we simply "adapt" to this "new reality." To this capitulation, Conservative Judaism says No! We must restore the Jewish communal will to promote the *mitzvah* of endogamy (in-marriage).

Experience has taught us that the only effective opposition to intermarriage today must be grounded in values and living based on the religious aspect of Judaism. This is no simple prescription. It requires Jews to change their lives in response to the crisis created by the growing rate of intermarriage. In essence, it requires personal religious renewal rather than changing *halakhah* (Jewish law). As seductive as untargeted "outreach" and patrilineal descent might be, they simply don't "cure" the illness we have. Unless Jewish continuity is infused with personal Jewish learning and Jewish living, it is a wasteful venture.

I suggest 10 priorities, evident within this volume, that can reverse the current trend. While the focus of these suggestions is the synagogue community, it is up to each and every one of us to ensure that this course of action is implemented.

First: We must revolutionize our thinking about Jewish education. Unfortunately, Jewish history, Jewish practice, Jewish thought, Bible, and liturgy have become irrelevant to the Hebrew school curriculum. We are not creating educated and practicing Jews. If that is our goal, we must be willing to restructure our synagogue schools and become more serious about the content learned in the classroom—because that is a major determinant of what comes out of the classroom.

Second: It makes no sense for children to learn Judaica in the synagogue and then go home to parents who may be uneducated, apathetic, or negative. Our synagogues must regard the "client" as the entire family. We must implement family education on a serious level.

Third: Day schools work, yet we are often too reluctant to promote them. We must encourage families to send their children to day schools. And the Conservative movement must begin to seriously establish networks of Solomon Schechter high schools.

Fourth: We must make certain that participation in informal education programs such as United Synagogue Youth (USY) become expectations in our synagogues—just as religious school is the norm. To be most effective, these programs must have talented advisors and youth directors. Also, if you wish to create strong bonds of Jewish identity, it is important to invest money in sending our youth to USY conventions, *kinnusim*, encampments, summer programs, and Jewish camps such as Ramah.

Fifth: We must develop within each synagogue the means by which each teenager, before graduation from high school, spends a summer in Israel. We must create financial incentives to make it possible. Equally important, we must invest the energy to actively recruit participation. No longer can we permit the Israel trip to be an optional activity.

Sixth: We must be more pro-active in reaching out to college students in whom we have invested such time, energy, and financial resources during their formative years. KOACH (Conservative Judaism's college-age programming) will help. Communal contact with collegians while they are away at school will have an impact. And involving college students in programming when they are home during vacations can also make a difference.

Seventh: We must remember that every single Jewish adult is at risk of intermarriage. We must develop programs specifically for this group and do more to make singles feel comfortable in the synagogue community.

Eighth: We must spread the message to congregants of all ages—Date only Jews! Marry only Jews! We must be prepared to speak out about the value of Jewish living and Jewish home life. Singles must understand and appreciate what they will be missing if they intermarry.

Ninth: We must make it normative for parents, grandparents, and friends to say no to intermarriage and interdating. We must make it acceptable for individuals to voice their displeasure. Just as we need support groups for parents whose children have intermarried, so too do we need groups for parents whose children are dating or close to marriage, to help them give the proper message to their children.

Tenth: Finally, we must tell parents the truth. There are no guarantees that intermarriage will not occur, but there are proven and effective safeguards. We have to tell them that, if they want to help prevent intermarriage, they must insist that their children take Jewish education seriously. They must insist that their children continue their Jewish education through high school. They must insist that their children become active in USY. They must help create a Jewish life in their homes that their children will want to emulate.

Our young people have taken a good step forward. In an attempt to change the psychological and sociological climate, our own USY changed its constitution to require international USY leaders to refrain from interdating. The teenagers realized that they have a contribution to make, influencing not only their fellow USYers but also the general climate of opinion in the Jewish community.

As we reflect on the CJF survey, we know that it is helpful in painting a picture of what is. But surveys are like snapshots. They reflect the present, and if surveys are good, they can give us a beautiful picture as to the current state of affairs. The problem arises when we let surveys predict the future. The tragedy in the Jewish community today is that American Jews are responding to the survey by wringing their hands when we should be working to correct the problem. The truth is that we can reverse the trend. We have the power. We know what to do. The test of our commitment is only in our willingness to do what we know must be done.

Yes, the rate of intermarriage is rising. The question we must confront is whether that statement of reality will change us—or whether we will try to change the reality. The choice is ours. This volume is intended to help us make the correct decision.

Acknowledgments

I am indebted to the Leadership Council of Conservative Judaism and its constituent organizations: the Jewish Theological Seminary, the Rabbinical Assembly, the United Synagogue for Conservative Judaism, the Women's League for Conservative Judaism, and the Federation of Jewish Men's Clubs, as well as to Jason Aronson Inc., publisher, for their assistance and support in making this volume a reality.

In particular I wish to acknowledge the crucial involvement of the following individuals: to Dr. Robert Abramson of the United Synagogue and to Rhonda Kahn of Women's League for thorough and insightful editorial work and substantive input; to Rabbi Gerald Zelizer of the Rabbinical Assembly for careful reading and suggestions; to Marilyn Henry and to Muriel Jorgensen for superb copy editing; to Alan Ades, Mark Sternfeld, and other lay leaders of the United Synagogue for encouragement; to the many members of Congregation Agudath Israel in Caldwell, New Jersey, for reading and critiquing the manuscript from the point of view of our laity; and to Rabbi Charles Simon of the Federation of Jewish Men's Clubs and Arthur Kurzweil of Jason Aronson Inc. for bringing this material to the public-at-large.

Finally, I want to thank my wonderfully supportive family for their love and understanding during my countless hours of involvement in composing and reediting this material: to my parents, Sol and Doris Silverstein; to my mother-in-law, Cili Neufeld, and father-in-law, Sol Neufeld, of blessed memory; to my children, David and Rebecca; and most of all to my wife, Rita.

Introduction

At a conference of the Young Leadership Division of the United Jewish Appeal, Professor Reuven Kimmelman of Brandeis University conducted an illustrative exercise. He asked persons whose parents were both born in the United States to raise their hands. He then requested that only persons whose four grandparents were American-born keep their hands lifted. Only a tiny percentage of those at the Spring 1994 conference met the profile of three complete generations in the United States. The obvious conclusion drawn by Dr. Kimmelman was that American Jewry is a community of immigrants and the children and grandchildren of immigrants.

This demographic reality should not be the case. After all, as early as 1880 there were 250,000 Jews, primarily of German descent, in North America. By natural progression, this quarter-million Jews should have more than 3 million Jewish descendants by 1990. They should represent at least one-third of the American Jewish population. But most of their great-grandchildren are not Jewish. And this gap in Jewish continuity was not the result of oppression or of anti-Semitism, but rather of interfaith marriage. In this wonderful, hospitable land, by the third generation, European Jews had lost the ability to articulate to their offspring why they should marry within the faith.

Sadly, this same process of erosion is happening once again within the families of American Jewry. This time, the 6 million, by and large Eastern European Jews who were identifiably Jewish in the 1950s, are watching their children and grandchildren drift away. Unless this trend is reversed or at least stemmed, by the year 2050 a future Professor Kimmelman will again find that most young Jews will be the children or grandchildren of Jewish immigrants who arrived in the United States after the 1950s.

What can be done? First and foremost, we must empower Jewish parents, Jewish single adults, Jewish teens, and Jewish religious and communal leaders to articulate Jewish continuity concerns when confronted with frequently posed questions. For example:

> Why be Jewish? What's the gain?
>
> What could possibly be wrong with interdating? It is merely having a good time.
>
> Where in the Torah or other Jewish sources does Judaism encourage marriage within the faith?
>
> If I fall in love with and marry a non-Jew, isn't it reasonable to assume that he/she will convert to Judaism?
>
> Even if my spouse does not convert, can't I raise my children to be Jews anyway?
>
> Is it racist, undemocratic, un-American to limit our dating and/or marital partners?
>
> If I'm not religiously observant, wouldn't I be a hypocrite to oppose my child's interdating/intermarriage?
>
> How can I reconcile my acceptance of intermarried relatives within our extended family while urging my children to marry within the faith?
>
> What difference does it make anyway? Are not Judaism and Christianity merely variations on the same theme of believing in God and being a good person?
>
> Are messianic Judaism, Unitarianism, Ethical Culture, Scientology, and other options viable alternatives for me as a intermarried Jew?

This volume offers answers to these and many other questions that arise from interfaith marriage. The material is intended for Jewish people of all stages of life and at all levels of religious practice. It is intended to empower American Jews to seriously identify and confront the problems intermarriage poses to Jewish continuity. Individual chapters are available as separate booklets from the United Synagogue Book Service.

As an American rabbi alarmed about the future of Jewish families in the United States, I urge you to carefully consider these issues. If additional questions not covered in this volume arise, I would welcome your correspondence, so that subsequent editions can incorporate the recommendations of serious readers.

Paraphrasing the words that *Ethics of Our Fathers* taught millennia ago: Although it is not up to us to complete awesome tasks, we are not permitted to be intimidated by the challenge and remain inactive. Instead, we must begin the process of renewal.

Please join with me and with the leadership institutions of Conservative Judaism in beginning a process of ensuring the Jewish future of our descendants.

1

Grounds for Concern:
Jewish Views of Intermarriage

The problem of transmitting our Jewishness to future generations is more challenging and crucial than ever. Our grandparents and other generations of immigrants encountered an American culture that was neatly divided into ethnic, religious, and racial groups. As late as 1960, Asian Americans routinely married one another, as did Italian and other white ethnic Protestants and Catholics, and American blacks and Hispanics. Within this socially differentiated pattern, American Jews predictably married one another as well.

Three decades later, little more than a generation later, people are crossing racial, religious, and ethnic lines to marry. And so it is with the Jews. More than 50 percent of young Jews are marrying persons of different backgrounds.

This demographic momentum poses a clear challenge to Jewish continuity. In the overwhelming majority of these intermarriages, the non-Jewish partner does not convert to Judaism. And in nearly three-quarters of these interfaith homes, the children are not being raised as Jews.

Also frightening is the fact that 90 percent of young adults who are "raised as Jews" in such interfaith homes do not have any sense of close ties to fellow Jews, or to the State of Israel, or to aiding Jews in distress, or to affiliating with a synagogue or any other type of Jewish organization. Neither, they say, are they interested in raising their own children as Jews. In all likelihood, within three generations, the descendants of intermarriage will disappear within the undifferentiated mass of American Christianity.

The demographic problems are compounded by cultural messages that militate against effectively raising our children as identifying Jews. We have to compete both with the Christian message that Judaism is a minority religion and with secularism's subtle denigration of all forms of organized religion.

Some messages of American culture are harmful not only to religion in general, but to Judaism in particular. At the 1992 General Assembly of the Council of Jewish Federations, Professor Arnold Eisen offered the following observations:

> We are struggling to reach Jews with the riches of meaning stored up in our tradition, in the context of a culture that generally thinks of . . . all or nothing. . . . We are attempting to join Jews together in ties that bind, to link them to their people and their tradition . . . in the face of unprecedented emphasis [solely] upon self-fulfillment . . . a challenge that any sort of Jewishness, of Yiddishkeit, whatever, must overcome.
>
> The difficulty we face is clear. Where once Jewish identity and commitment and community could be taken for granted—in fact, they were nearly impossible to escape—we must now argue for every Jewish soul at every moment, must persuade every mind, must cajole and entice every heart.

The first step in our battle in the fight for Jewish continuity is the fight against intermarriage.

1. Rabbi, throughout my years in Hebrew school and Jewish youth groups, no one ever showed me where Jewish sacred

texts oppose intermarriage. From my perspective, it seems as though such stubbornness is simply parental narrow-mindedness and that it has no basis in Jewish religion.

You are correct that Hebrew schools and Jewish youth groups have been remiss in omitting text-based discussions of Judaism's opposition to interfaith marriage. Nevertheless, such sacred sources abound and merit some elaboration.

In Deuteronomy 7:3–4, we read the following prohibition:

> You shall not marry with your non-Jewish neighbors; your daughter shall not be given to their son, nor their daughter to your son. For intermarriage will turn your children away from Judaism, and they will end up serving other religions.

Numerous other biblical verses repeat this theme, notably Exodus 34:14–16, Ezra 10:10–12, Nehemiah 10:30–31, and Malachi 2:11–12.

Moreover, sacred Jewish literature throughout the ages reiterates such concerns. The Talmud, in Tractate *Avodah Zarah* 36b, for example, cautions against drinking non-Jewish wine in (mixed) social settings because it would lead to potential romance and ultimately intermarriage. Similarly, the fundamental code of Jewish law, the *Shulhan Arukh, Yoreh De'ah* 114, prohibits "breaking" non-Jewish bread as part of a social precaution "due to intermarriage," because a person who comes to break bread with non-Jews will eat with them and might ultimately intermarry with them. Similarly, the central Jewish mystical text, the *Zohar, Shemot* 36, reflects:

> There are three persons who drive away God's presence from the Jewish world . . . [the second of the three is] he who cohabits with the daughter of a Gentile. . . . [Moreover] the leaders of the people in each generation are punished for this transgression if they are aware [of it] and are not zealous [to prevent intermarriage].

Furthermore, in the Midrash, the biblical patriarch Isaac's blindness is traced to the stress and unhappiness he experienced in connection with his son Esau's intermarriages to Hittite women. These legends claim that God brought blindness to Isaac in order to salve the pain he felt every time he noticed the smoke of idolatry arising from Esau's home or saw Esau engaging in idolatrous practices (*Midrash Tanhuma, Toledot* 7). In a similar fashion, the commentary of Samson Raphael Hirsch in 19th-century Germany faulted Esau's mixed marriages with yielding the irreparable divisions in the family of Isaac and Rebecca.

> By intermarrying, Hirsch contends, Esau became a house divided between Abraham's belief in one spiritual God and the many idol-gods of his wives. This disqualified him from inheriting the leadership of the Jewish people from Abraham. Hirsch reasons that a home where two religions are practiced or where two religious traditions are practiced or where there is not a joint commitment to a single faith by both parents is often the cause of confusion, misunderstanding, and trouble between parents and children. (Harvey J. Fields, *A Torah Commentary for Our Times—Volume 1: Genesis, Parshat Toledot*, p. 69)

All traditional Jewish commentators throughout the ages reaffirmed the Torah and Jewish law code prohibition, "Thou shalt not intermarry." By no means does this represent narrow-mindedness on the part of the Torah toward non-Jews. To the contrary, the Five Books of Moses are replete with universal values and messages of fair treatment of Gentiles. Nevertheless, Jewish textual opposition to intermarriage is a recognition that out-marriage will jeopardize the future of the Jewish people, the bearers of God's Torah. As any objective assessment confirms, Jewish continuity requires in-marriage! Thus, Jewish sacred literature throughout the ages, committed to Jewish survival, has continually advocated such a practical imperative.

2. Okay, Rabbi, perhaps individual verses in the Bible and Jewish law prohibited interfaith marriage; however, many of the great ancient Jewish leaders such as Moses and Joseph clearly disregarded these strictures.

Once again, you are correct. However, the Jewish tradition draws a different set of conclusions from the stories of individual aberrant behavior contained in our holy writings. Both Moses and Joseph are instances of young single Jews who were separated from the Jewish community, thereby becoming prey to assimilation and intermarriage. Most of those who intermarried in ancient times, as well as their descendants, were totally lost to the Jewish tradition—as occurred with Ishmael and Esau, sons of Abraham and of Isaac, respectively.

> And Ishmael settled in the wilderness of Paran. His mother, Hagar, arranged for an Egyptian wife for him. (Genesis 21:21)
>
> And when Esau was 40 years old, he took a Hittite woman as his wife. This caused a bitterness of spirit for his parents Isaac and Rebecca. (Genesis 26:34–35)

Thus, the significance of the Moses and Joseph stories is not that they intermarried; rather, they represented rare cases of Jews seemingly lost to the tradition who were miraculously reclaimed due to unique circumstances of divine intervention.

The biblical concern about out-marriage is reflected as well by numerous other episodes. The most explicit, of course, is the deliberate effort of Abraham, the first Jew, to find a suitable wife for his heir, Isaac. This is described in elaborate detail in Genesis, chapter 24. The subsequent matchmaking mission by his servant Eliezer results in the pairing of Isaac with Rebecca. Similarly overt is Rebecca's comment to Isaac:

> I am scared to death about the Gentile daughters of this area. If our son Jacob takes one of these girls as a wife, my life and legacy will no longer have any value. (Genesis 27:46)

Consequently, Jacob is sent to the home of his uncle, Laban, where he ultimately marries Leah and Rachel. Such tales of the peril of intermarriage are found throughout the later sections of the Bible, particularly in relation to the days of King Solomon and of Ezra. The biblical record of opposing interfaith marriage is quite clear and consistent.

3. Rabbi, perhaps Jewish sources oppose intermarriage and postulate that an intermarrying Jew and his/her descendants will be lost to Judaism, but can't I resolve this problem by marrying a non-Jewish person and having that individual convert to Judaism?

It is certainly valid to observe that a significant number of converts have entered into contemporary Jewish life and have become a true blessing to the Jewish community. Some of our most active families are conversionary families in which the sincerity and piety of Jews by Choice and their born-Jewish spouses have inspired other Jews by Birth as well. This is analogous to the blessing that the former Gentile members of the family of Moses and the family of Joseph ultimately came to represent for the Jewish communities of their day. However, the problem with this plan of action is whether it is likely to occur. Just as the reclaiming of the households of Moses and of Joseph in biblical times were extraordinary and rare events among the multitudes of the intermarried, so, too, are actively involved conversionary households rare among the vast numbers of American Jewish intermarrieds.

The National Jewish Population Survey of 1990, for instance, documents that nearly 95 percent of Gentile spouses of Jews in interfaith marriages occurring during the period 1985–1990 *did not convert into Judaism*. The remaining 5 percent who did claim conversion include a substantial number of persons who never underwent a formal period of study or a religious ceremony, whether Reform, Conservative, Orthodox, or Reconstruction-ist. It also includes some formal converts whose motivations were insincere, others who later reverted to Christianity, and still others whose initial sincerity became tainted by the indifference to Judaism displayed by their born-Jewish partner and his/her Jewish family members. Insincere and/or dissatisfied converts must be regarded with grave caution. They simply will not create a Jewish home atmosphere transferable to future offspring. A household with a Jewishly ambivalent convert, accompanied by Christian in-laws and a Christian extended family, will not likely result in producing Jewishly identifying children. The assumption that Jewish continuity can be assured by transforming intermarriage into a conversionary family is usually wishful thinking and offers Jewish leadership serious grounds for concern.

4. If my non-Jewish spouse does not convert to Judaism, can't I still perpetuate Judaism by raising my children as Jews?

Here, too, the goal is praiseworthy, but the likelihood of success is remote. In the same 1990 nationwide survey, we learned that 72 percent of the children raised in intermarried homes in which the Gentile partner has not converted to Judaism *are not raised as Jewish children*. Furthermore, among the 28 percent of sons and daughters who are considered by their parents to be Jewish, many receive no Jewish education, exhibit no identifiable pattern of Jewish observance, and do not meaningfully identify with the Jewish community, locally, nationally, or worldwide.

The consequences of a two-faith household are underscored by the 1983 study entitled *Children of Intermarriage* conducted by Dr. Egon Mayer on behalf of the American Jewish Committee. In this unique scientific evaluation of the attitudes of adult sons and daughters reared as Jews within a mixed marriage, a series of conclusions validate our concern. In addition to the virtual disappearance of any level of Jewish observance (i.e., *Shabbat*, *kashrut*, Jewish holidays, and synagogue affiliation), residual traces of Jewish identity faded as well.

Of the respondents, 83 percent perceived "no greater responsibility to fellow Jews than to others in need." The simple act "of belonging to a Jewish community" was deemed "unimportant" by 81 percent. Eighty percent received no formal Jewish education. Whereas less than 25 percent annually light Hanukkah candles or attend a Passover *seder*, more than 80 percent help decorate a Christmas tree and participate in the exchange of Christmas gifts.

Only 18 percent agree with the statement, "Being Jewish is very important to me." Barely 26 percent would either "definitely" or "probably" want to be Jewish if given the chance of being born once again into this world. Just 30 percent expressed any special "responsibility to support" the State of Israel. Only 11 percent would be "very upset" if their sons and daughters "did not regard themselves as Jews." Finally and not surprisingly, virtually none (just 3 percent) "would discourage" their offspring "from marrying someone who is not Jewish."

These difficulties have not been mitigated by the Reform movement's "patrilineal" proclamation of 1983, which offers Reform Jewish status to the child of a Jewish man and a non-Jewish woman without requiring the youngster's formal conversion. Such an approach is problematic in many ways. First, it is a departure from the standards practiced by every other Jewish community throughout the world, throughout the ages, and among Conservative and Orthodox Jews in the United States. Second, it is a deterrent against the sincere conversion by one's non-Jewish spouse and children. Third, it has been misunderstood by the mass media and the American Jewish population at large. Most Jews assume that patrilinealism means simply declaring one's child to be a Jew. In actuality, however, even for Reform Judaism, patrilineal status requires a *bris* (ritual circumcision) or baby-naming at birth, religious school education, *bar/bat mitzvah*, and confirmation ceremonies. Among mixed-marrieds, such commitment is increasingly rare.

With such data in mind, it is not unexpected that in community surveys such as the 1980s study of Philadelphia Jewry researchers could not find a single case of mixed marriage (without conversion of the non-Jewish partner) in which the grandchildren of such a couple had remained Jewish in their adult years. Such a familiar and depressing process of disappearance via assimilation already occurred for the Sephardic families who were the founders of American Jewish communities, as well as for a high percentage of early and mid-19th-century German Jewish families within the United States. Descendants of mixed Jewish-Christian marriages in an overwhelmingly Christian society inevitably leave the Jewish fold by the third or fourth generation.

Thus, a proposed "solution" of harmonizing intermarriage and Jewish survival by "raising the children as Jews" is statistically possible in our current era of 5 million American Jews, but over several generations it is unlikely to succeed. This approach, too, represents serious grounds for concern.

5. Why not raise my future offspring without any religion at all?

Religion provides a vocabulary of values. Family, church and synagogue, through their principles and rituals, are critical in teaching morality to young children, especially in a society where schooling is often secular and "value-free." In *The Intermarriage Handbook*, researchers Judy Petsonk and Jim Remsen have assessed: "For many children, and for many adults, religion is an important part of . . . self-definition. Religion gives people a common history, values, traditions, rituals, stories, jokes. This shared system gives them an anchor in the world – an identity" (p. 193). Thus, the avoidance of a religious dimension may create a void in a person's healthy emotional/ psychological/spiritual development. As typically indicated by a young woman named Mary, a product of an interfaith home: "[In my parents' home] religion was avoided like the plague . . . because [it] would open up a Pandora's box. . . . Thus I grew up confused over what I was supposed to do about religion" (Steven Carr Reuben, *Raising Jewish Children in a Contemporary World*, pp. 116–117).

A religious identity will be critical to most children throughout life. They will need some rituals associated with the birth of children, reaching adolescence, marriage, and coping with death. They will require some concepts of religion to deal with faith concerns at moments of illness or crisis, of joy or of personal spiritual awareness, of medical/ethical issues ranging from abortion and birth control to organ donations and terminating life-support systems.

As an adult offspring of a dual-faith home told the Union of American Hebrew Congregations (UAHC): "Don't make your kid feel like she is nothing. Everybody wants to be something [specific], to be called something [specific], and it isn't good to be nothing."

6. Why not raise the children in both Judaism and Christianity?

While Judaism and Christianity each make vital contributions to spirituality, they possess their own integrity and distinct religious messages. Therefore, raising children "in both" may present many problems to the children's development. Already by ages 3 to 5, our children become old enough to ask and to be sensitive to religious questions, and we have to be comfortable with consistent, rather than contradictory, answers. What happened to Grandpa, now that he died? Do we believe that abortion is okay? Are we in favor of organ donations? Is it all right to disconnect life-support systems to a terminally ill patient? Where is God? What is my religion? How come there are different religions? What happens to good people who are not Christians or not Jewish? Who created the world? What are miracles? Therapist Lena Romanoff has commented:

> Questions such as 9-year-old Brandon Perez's are telling—and not uncommon. "If I'm Jewish, then how can I believe in Jesus?" he asked his parents. "And if I'm Catholic, how can I not believe in Jesus? Do I believe in him on Sunday but not on Saturday?" (Lena Romanoff, *Your People, My People*, p. 53)

Under the best of circumstances, these are difficult questions to answer. They are the types of questions often brought to the local rabbi, priest, or minister. However, without a unified and confident response from parents and/or religious schools or clergy, a child's inquisitiveness is answered only with "Mom and Dad do not agree on this" (causing a loyalty conflict) or "There is no answer" (creating confusion).

Like Judaism (Reform, Conservative, Reconstructionist, Orthodox), Christianity includes an extraordinarily diverse range of faith groups (Evangelical Protestants, mainline Protestants, Eastern Orthodox, Roman Catholics). Since Jewish, Catholic, and Protestant beliefs frequently are at odds, artificially combined Jewish-Christian responses to these inquiries will not suffice. Our offspring cannot be instructed to both believe that God is One (the *Shema*) and that there is a divine Trinity (Father, Son, Holy Ghost). A son or daughter cannot be taught to believe that Jesus was the son of God and the messiah (Christianity) and that Jesus was neither (Judaism). A child cannot meaningfully be told that infants are born with original sin (Catholics, Lutherans, Eastern Orthodox, Methodists, and

Presbyterians) and that babies are born totally without moral blemish (Judaism). Boys and girls cannot handle reading Christian scriptural passages asserting that the Jews killed Jesus, while at the same time studying to be good Jews themselves. We cannot effectively believe the claim of many Christian groups that Christianity (a *new* testament) has superseded ancient Judaism (an *old* testament) while simultaneously affirming the Torah (Hebrew scripture) as central to Jewish life. Moreover, a youngster should not be instructed that only members of one's own religious group can be "saved" in heaven when they die (Evangelicals) and at the same time be informed that all ethical persons of all religious groups will be rewarded by God in the hereafter (Judaism and some liberal Christian denominations).

I went home from (Baptist) Sunday school one day and cried as I told my mother that the teacher had said that the Jews—which I took to include my Jewish father—were going to hell because they didn't believe in Jesus. (A painful incident related by Eloise, a retired teacher, raised in two religions; see Leslie Goodman-Malamuth and Robin Margolis, *Between Two Worlds*, p. 21)

School psychologist Dr. David Yammer has observed:

Children can be taught that different people or peoples believe contradictory Jewish vs. Christian statements. It is when they are taught that they are expected to feel comfortable "living the contradiction" that conflict and/or confusion arises. We have a natural tendency to avoid cognitive dissonance. Asking a child to live with ongoing dissonance is asking a lot.

We cannot expect a child to be able to be serious about both religions at the same time. Children do better when parents have done the work necessary to present relatively consistent responses to "what our family believes."

7. Why not expose sons and daughters to both Judaism and Christianity during childhood and let them make their own choice later in life?

Some parents assume that by giving children exposure to both religions, it will best be left to these sons or daughters to later choose one of the two faiths for themselves. Such passing of responsibility onto the shoulders of the youngsters is unfair. It is a parental cop-out. Adults raised in mixed-marriage settings stressed to interviewer Charlotte Anker:

> Letting the children choose puts them in the position of having to reject one parent or the other. [As one woman said to Anker] "No matter how prepared they think they are, parents often freak out when this happens. They become enraged to see their children become devout Jews or Christians.
>
> "My mother always said I could be what I want to be, but when I became Jewish she got terribly upset," is a typical statement. "Sometimes under the pressure, the children go off and become Buddhists—then both parents feel rejected.". . .
>
> A significant number of [adult offspring of mixed marriage] . . . refuse to affiliate with any religion because they cannot bear to choose between parents. (Charlotte Anker, "We are the Children You Warned Our Parents About," p. 37)

Other adult children of intermarriage raised to make their own choice of religious affiliation emulate their parents, pushing off this decision upon someone else. Specifically, many young women attempt to resolve the issue of divided loyalties to parents by planning to assume the religion of the man they marry. One offspring of such a home said:

> It was almost like my life was coming to this, having a Southern boyfriend and a Jewish boyfriend, my mother's part of the country and my father's religion. . . . I had to actually say to myself,

"What am I gonna choose? Am I gonna get mixed up with this
Southerner and go live in the South and become a Southerner, or
go with this Jew and become a Jew?" (Judy Petsonk and Jim
Remsen, *The Intermarriage Handbook*, p. 200)

Moreover, adult sons and daughters of households who
have deferred religious issues tend to be either uneasy about
affiliating with any organized religion whatsoever or consciously choose a religion distant from both parents.

It is unfair to expect a child to decide upon a religion. The
Rev. Ronald Osbourne, chaplain at the University of Iowa, has
written: "What happens [in such situations] is that the children are not exposed to either religious tradition sufficiently to
feel religious meanings from the inside out. Since religion is
caught, not taught, it is never caught. They, in fact, are raised
as [nothing]" ("Marriage of Christians and Jews," p.11). Neither two religions vaguely harmonized nor the absence of
religion altogether will be a viable lifelong solution for one's
son or daughter. Painfully unresolved religious issues may
end up being passed on to the next generation, like the baton
in a relay race.

Parents must select one specific religion. They should not
leave their sons' and daughters' religious tutelage to chance.
Nor should aspects of Judaism and Christianity be randomly
thrust upon children. These two traditions are not merely
variations of the same theme. They represent fundamentally
different lenses through which to view birth, adolescence,
marriage, adulthood, and death. They offer distinctive practices, holidays, beliefs, symbols, and rituals. They each present unique views of God, sin, repentance, the messiah, life
after death, and other religious beliefs. They provide separate
frameworks with which to deal with contemporary ethical
dilemmas ranging from abortion, fertility drugs, and surrogate motherhood to organ transplants, living wills, and disconnecting life-support systems.

After interviewing 60 adult offspring of intermarriage, Paul and Rachel Cowan concluded:

> Both those who praised their parents and those who criticized them conveyed the same message. They valued clarity and a sense of security. They felt parents should choose a religious identity for their children and not leave it up to them to choose. Furthermore, they thought parents should furnish an environment in which the children would feel comfortable living with that identity. (Paul and Rachel Cowan, *Mixed Blessings: Marriage Between Jews and Christians*, p. 247)

Parents decide where to live, what schools to attend, which medical group to visit. Parents also should decide for their children (preferably before the parents marry) which religion is most suitable. As parents, we owe our children a clear statement regarding their religious upbringing.

8. Regardless of these considerations, can't I have a fine marital relationship anyway?

Clearly, a fine marital relationship is possible within the context of a mixed marriage. Here, too, however, the risks are quite high. Divorce has become ever more common within society at large and creates enormous personal anguish for husband, wife, children, and in-laws. Couples consisting of two Jewish partners currently divorce at an alarming rate of approximately 15 percent. These relatively modest statistics are related to the effectiveness of the Jewish tradition and of shared Jewish values in cementing the marital bond. Regrettably, the 15-percent figure is dwarfed by the 40- to 50-percent frequency of marital break-up for intermarrieds. Lacking the commonality of religious assumptions, lingering bitterness in such cases is frequently intense. Custody battles are complicated by broken promises regarding the religion in which children will be reared when some divorced people who were insincere converts into Judaism (i.e., those who converted solely for the sake of marriage) lapse into their former faith.

The marital instability of interfaith marriage is related to what Paul and Rachel Cowan aptly label "time bombs." These can unexpectedly disrupt romance. An interfaith couple, infatuated with one another, often encounters family opposition but rarely anticipates the powerful disruptive pull that religious feelings and traditions can have at times of birth, death, tragedy, ethnic tension, and so on. While such marriages initially hide self-doubt and questioning beneath the surface, these submerged issues are ever ready to rise to the fore. The Cowans discuss these "time bombs" in their admonitions to couples who are contemplating mixed marriage, but plan to avoid religious issues:

> What will happen when the stakes get higher? Right now your disagreements are theoretical. But when "time bombs" occur? When the baby is born, what will you decide? *Bris*—baptism—neither? Raised as a Christian, a Jew, a . . . ?
>
> Does raising a child as a Jew or as a Christian involve more than simply visiting grandparents for major holidays? If so, what does it involve? Study at home? A more formal religious education? If so, where? At a church or at a synagogue? If that decision is made, will both parents participate in it? And what kind of coming of age does each parent envisage? A bar mitzvah? A confirmation in a church? (Paul and Rachel Cowan, *Mixed Blessings*, p. 186)

Given all of this potential for anguish, is it any wonder that survey data indicates the great reluctance of many mixed-marrieds to have children at all, or the tendency to postpone this potentially destabilizing change!

Furthermore, even before the arrival of children, such "time bombs" may explode in a mixed marriage, as issues of profound meaning surface. The Cowans ask those considering

intermarriage if they have ever thought of death, their partner's or their own: "How will you cope with death? Jewish
shiva, Catholic wake, Protestant funeral? Can you be buried
together? Who will say *Kaddish* for you?" (Paul and Rachel
Cowan, *Mixed Blessings*, p. 186).

Similarly, Dennis Prager and Joseph Telushkin point out in
Nine Questions People Ask About Judaism: "Chances are that
being Jewish means more, perhaps much more, to you than
you think. And it is eminently possible that in the near future
it will come to mean far more than at present" (p. 141).

If a war breaks out in Israel, or a swastika is painted on the
local synagogue, or the Ku Klux Klan holds a heavily pub-
licized rally, a submerged sense of Jewish identity may exhibit
itself in a fashion far more forceful than might have been
expected or than a non-Jewish spouse may understand. Similarly, a Jewish partner's discomfort within Christian settings
may prove more powerful than previously contemplated. As
Philip Roth wrote in his semiautobiographical novel *The
Counterlife*:

> It never fails. I am never more of a Jew than I am in a church when
> the organ begins. I may be estranged at the Wailing Wall but
> without being a stranger. . . . But between me and church devo-
> tion there is an unbridgeable world of feeling, a natural and
> thoroughgoing incompatibility. I have the emotions of a spy in the
> adversary's camp and feel I'm overseeing the very rites that em-
> body the ideology that's been responsible for the persecution and
> mistreatment of Jews. (p. 256)

On a very personal level, Jewish partners in a mixed marriage often feel personally "violated" by having a Christmas
tree, adorned with Christological symbols, within their own
homes. For many Jews, what to Christians is an innocent
"tree" brings to mind intense inner feelings of exclusion, of
anti-Semitism, of persecution. The appearance of this visceral

symbol of the Christian cross, the wood of Jesus's crucifixion, is yet one more potential "time bomb" among the large arsenal of events that can explode in a mixed marriage. Moreover, additional cultural gaps, often requiring "ethnotherapy" by social workers, often divide mixed couples over questions of child-rearing styles, closeness to extended family, the use of money, view of the appropriate use of alcoholic beverages, birth control, abortion, disconnecting life-support systems for the comatose/terminally ill, and so on.

For all of the above reasons, mixed marriages are more prone to break up. Pressures from in-laws, friends, and associates become more complex and potentially explosive. Normal life-cycle milestones, which traditionally enrich marital bonds, become laden with tension. Common husband–wife misunderstandings may evoke reactions of anti-Semitism or anti-"goyish" (Gentile) stereotyping that further complicate resolution. Clearly, such households require unusual doses of patience and maturity, beyond what might be expected from most couples. Given the pain and anguish that result from such divorces and divisive custody battles, here too we have grounds for concern.

9. Well, at least one thing is for certain. Even if I intermarry and my spouse does not convert, and my children are not certain to be Jews, of course my own Judaism remains assured.

In this dimension, as well, we are quite alarmed. The 1990 National Jewish Population Survey has shocked American Jews into the realization that Jewish partners in intermarriages are possible losses to Judaism. The data indicated, for example, that more than 210,000 born Jews in the United States have converted to other religions, cults, or creeds (i.e. born-again Christianity, Roman Catholicism, mainline Protestantism, Jews for Jesus, Unitarianism, Scientology, etc.). This figure is so large that it exceeds the number of non-Jewish spouses who have converted into our ranks. It includes many intermarried born Jews. In addition, a further contingent of 1.1 million born Jews no longer consider themselves to be identified with any religion whatsoever. Foremost among this latter category are intermarried Jews who come to feel that the easiest way to cope with the disharmony caused by two competing religious traditions is to become totally secular, to identify religiously as "nothing."

Formal conversion out of Judaism or simply considering oneself as "nothing," leads the intermarried Jew not only to be uninvolved in the synagogue and in Jewish communal life, but it is frequently also accompanied by a distancing from Jewish friends and Jewish family members. There is every reason for us to fear that the warning offered in Deuteronomy 7:3–4 — that the intermarried Jew will "serve other religions" — has come to be true in our day, as it has been throughout Jewish history. Interfaith marriage not only removes future generations from the Jewish fold; it also leads to the gradual erosion of the Jewish identity of the mixed-married Jew. Although exceptions do exist, a gradual process of alienation is greatly to be feared. Here, too, we have grounds for concern.

10. I can agree that becoming a Catholic or a Protestant means leaving the fold. What about Messianic Judaism as a compromise choice?

Your question is reflective of some widely held misconceptions about alleged compromise positions between Christianity and Judaism. To assume that entry into Jews for Jesus does not involve an exodus from Judaism is to fall into a clever ideological trap.

Messianic Judaism *is* Evangelical Christian proselytizing to the Jews. The founder of Jews for Jesus, a deceptive proselytizing technique, was Martin Rosen, a former Jew who converted to Evangelical Christianity in the mid-1950s. Rosen was ordained as a Baptist minister in 1957 and was assigned to serve the American Board of Missions (missionaries) to the Jews. In this capacity Rev. Rosen became sensitized to the theological vulnerability of many American Jews. When approaching those who knew little about Jewish belief, Rosen represented himself to them as an "authentic Jew," Moishe Rosen. Yet even the most assimilated Jews resisted formal conversion out of Judaism.

By 1970, Rosen developed a solution to his dilemma, for which he was able to obtain Baptist backing and funding. Dov Aharoni Fisch writes:

> [Rosen was able to] synthesize a new missionary ideology, based on his earlier successes in confusing young Jews [largely] from non-observant homes by asserting that it was he who was the authentic Jew, not their rabbis. Summoning all of [his ample] . . . marketing skills, he decided to send forth [from his base in San Francisco] individuals portraying themselves as "Jews made kosher by Jesus." Preying on the lack of Jewish knowledge . . . Rosen would claim that his movement was not less Jewish than the typical Reform or Conservative Jewish temple [e.g., it was just one more Jewish denomination]. To help reinforce this deception, Rosen's evangelists occasionally would wear yarmulkas (skullcaps) or other Jewish symbols [tallis, Hebrew names of the "congregation," Torah scrolls, menorahs, matzah, etc.]. (Dov Aharoni Fisch, *Jews for Nothing*, p. 26)

Over the last 20 years, Rosen's fledgling efforts have grown into a full-blown Christian missionary effort called Messianic Judaism. Misleading advertisements are targeted at Russian, Iranian, Israeli, and other immigrant Jews arriving in America, as well as toward the alienated and *intermarried* among native-born Jews. Free admission is offered for "High Holiday Services," "Passover *seders*," "Jewish Day Camp and/or Child

Care," "Hebrew Song Concerts," and other recruitment events. Guidelines for missionaries include the following:

> Words that elicit strong negative reactions among Jews [are] . . . avoided at all costs—at least in initial stages of contact. Jesus [is renamed] . . . "Yeshua," Christ [becomes] . . . "Messiah," or better yet, the Hebrew "Mashiach," a Hebrew Christian [becomes] . . . "a Messianic Jew," baptism [becomes] . . . "immersion in the mikveh." The wearing of crosses and crucifixes [is] . . . strongly discouraged [instead] a Jewish star. . . . Most crucial [are] . . . the out-of-context memorization of purported messianic prophecies from the Hebrew Bible. (Larry Levey, "Why I Embraced, Then Rejected Messianic Judaism," p. 20)

Once ensnared by this bait, vulnerable Jews are met with classic, cult-like, communal "love-bombing" via intense interpersonal contact by trained missionary operatives. These Jews are gradually persuaded that one need not leave Judaism to become "completed as a Jew" through faith in Jesus and Christian doctrine. Of course, this is all fraught with intentional deceit. Dennis Prager has commented:

> There is no such thing as a "Jew for Jesus.". . . The deceit lies in the fact that these Jews who come to believe in Jesus as their God, Savior and Messiah do not acknowledge that they have become Christians. . . .
> The fact that the first Christians were Jews is pointless, since the first Mormons were Christians, the first Buddhists were Hindus, and the first Protestants were Catholics. Yet . . . Protestants [have not] called themselves "Catholics for No Pope" . . . and Jews do not demean Christianity or Judaism by calling [the tens of thousands of] Christians who convert to Judaism "Completed Christians" or "Christians without Christ."
> Why, then, among all religious groups in the world do some [Evangelical and missionizing] Christians believe that there can be

"Jews for Jesus?". . . . [Because] the only way to attract any [significant] number of Jews to Christianity is to deceive Jews who are ignorant of Judaism into believing that they can keep their Jewish identity while adopting Christian beliefs. (Dennis Prager, "Is There Such a Thing as 'Jews for Jesus'?" pp. 6–7)

Therefore, it is incorrect and indeed sacrilegious to assume that if you opt for so-called Messianic Judaism, you or your future children or spouse are doing anything other than converting out of Judaism and into Christianity.

11. What about Unitarianism as a neutral ground?

Unitarianism is Christianity. Some Jews wrongfully assume that Unitarianism is not a Christian faith. On this basis, they are persuaded to seek this neutral, middle path between Judaism and Christianity as a solution to their intermarriage religious dilemmas. Yet Unitarianism is Christianity! Do not be deceived. Judy Petsonk and Jim Remsen have surmised:

Unitarianism [is part of] Protestantism. . . . [Most] Unitarian congregations . . . have a definite Christian flavor to them. They [are] . . . called churches. Their officiants are known as ministers. They . . . sing hymns, have responsive [Christian] readings, refer frequently to Jesus, have a [Christian-style] invocation and benediction, perhaps offer a form of communion . . . a naming ceremony [for infants that is called] a christening. . . . Adolescents . . . are welcomed into membership through . . . confirmation. (*The Intermarriage Handbook*, pp. 272–273)

In addition, the heavily cerebral approach of Unitarianism, while appealing to some adults, is quite frustrating to future offspring. For most children, Unitarianism lacks the drama of Jewish ritual, with the sounding of the *shofar*, the multiple stimuli of the Passover *seder*, the warmth of the Hanukkah lights. Affiliating as a family with a Unitarian church is too bland to satisfy the religious needs of future sons and daughters. Furthermore

> [Unitarian churches] seem to have limitations as identities for children. There are few Unitarians . . . overall, so a child can easily feel isolated. Their intellectual thrust can be difficult for small children to grasp. It can be hard for a child to explain to peers what a Unitarian . . . is or believes. [And it does not have] . . . deep roots in history, or the coherent belief system which makes either Judaism or Catholicism [or mainstream Protestantism] such a powerful identity base. (*The Intermarriage Handbook*, p. 206)

12. Are there perils in a Jew selecting transcendental meditation as an alternative choice?

Transcendental meditation (T.M.) *is* an Eastern religion. Some intermarried Jews play out their spiritual needs in T.M., which they are told by initiates is nonreligious in nature. "Meditation is a general technique of concentrating one's consciousness on one point or idea, increasing the intensity and duration of this concentration until separation between self and non-self is overcome" (Elimelech Lamdan, "Judaism and Transcendental Meditation," p. 209).

Jews are informed that there is nothing inconsistent for a Jew to engage in T.M. while remaining Jewish. Rabbi Elimelech Lamdan posits that some naive Jews are drawn to T.M. due to its secrecy, its novelty, its apparent ease of access, and its misleading claim of simply offering techniques for enhancing one's awareness of oneself in lieu of a religious system.

At first glance, T.M. appears perfectly compatible with Judaism. At the elementary stages to which novices are first introduced, T.M. simply seems to be a technique and appears to make no mention of one's soul or faith. However, as one is brought into ever more serious encounter with this Hindu system, tutors probe the inner recesses of Eastern religious philosophies. Rabbi Lamdan writes:

> Our problem worsens when the [vulnerable] Jewish student of T.M. [unfamiliar with Jewish spirituality] becomes more curious and begins probing deeply into its philosophy. . . . He now accepts answers which, previous to his spiritual experiences with the Self [via T.M.], he would have scorned as "religious answers.". . . Not having a previous standard of [Jewish] spiritual experience with which to compare and evaluate [T.M.'s] answers, he tends to accept them uncritically. (Elimelech Lamdan, "Judaism and Transcendental Meditation," p. 214)

In actuality, transcendental meditation was originated by a Hindu religious luminary called Gurudev, the teacher of the current T.M. leader Maharishi Mahesh Yogi. New recruits are invited to lectures presenting T.M. in seemingly scientific and statistical terms. Interested students are then paired with a teacher, who will gradually tutor the novice in his own personal mantra (a sound or syllable) around which the T.M. discipline focuses. Initiation includes an offering to Gurudev, and a picture of Maharishi Mahesh Yogi is presented to the newcomer, to be hung on a wall over a small table that is to receive future student offerings. A flower, burning incense, as well as prayers of thanks to Gurudev and Maharishi are further components of the ritual. In its final stage of evolution, the T.M. practitioner is urged to practice the mantra repetition for 40 minutes a day. By this point, an elaborate religious ideology has been introduced.

> Focusing this mental energy [of meditation] into the depths of the soul, eliminating thereby the limitations of the ego and merging into the infinite being of God . . . [the first basic premise is] the

belief that man is a soul which is temporarily bound to a physical body in its earthly lifetime. A second basic premise is that this soul is inherently pure, peaceful, and complete, for it is part of the infinitude of God. The resulting conclusion is the third basic point: that man's purpose in life is to purify himself, and that can be accomplished by living a natural life in accordance with the nature of his soul and not with the outside physical world. Man must use his mind to direct his thoughts to the spiritual side of life and away from the physical. (Elimelech Lamdan, "Judaism and Transcendental Meditation," p. 209)

Once a person fully accepts the religious edicts of T.M., one has left Jewish religious life and has fully entered into Eastern religion.

13. What about turning instead to discipline of the mind such as Scientology?

Scientology is a cult. Scientology was started in 1950 by L. Ron Hubbard via a book entitled *Dianetics: The Modern Science of Mental Health*. Within five years, Scientology had become a religion with more than 4 million members, 22 churches, and 100 missions in 33 countries. Their ministers deliver sermons and preside over life-cycle ceremonies including christenings, weddings, and funerals. Scientology offers a theology with a concept of "Thetan," a spirit that lives on after death in another body. This Thetan, a "prime mover unmoved," is likened by Scientologists to God. Hubbard claims that Scientology is an extension of Buddhism. Hubbard is the Church's sole prophet. His wife, Mary Sue, holds the title of "Worldwide Guardian" of Scientology. Ministers are organized in different levels. Branches and missions are arranged in a hierarchy called "Orgs."

Recruiters into Scientology do not initially indicate that this ideology represents a distinct religious ideology. They simply tell prospective initiates that Scientology is a means to sharpen one's mental awareness, enhance one's ability to communicate, and improve one's physical health and spiritual serenity. They claim that newcomers need not abandon their previous religion to be a Scientologist. In particular, "The American Jewish Scientology Committee" organizes activities targeted at Jews both in North America and in Israel. Recruitment involves a four-step strategy:

> The first step is "contact," the initial friendly approach to the potential member. The second step is to "handle" the recruit, i.e., to overcome his reservations about Scientology. The third is to find the "ruin," or vulnerable area, of the potential member's life such as drugs, sex, a past crime, or incest. In the fourth step, "salvage," the recruiter assures the potential member that he knows other people who have overcome similar problems through Scientology. (James and Marcia Rudin, *Prison or Paradise: The New Religious Cults*, p. 87)

Recruits are enrolled in Scientology courses, leading gradually into ever more excessive expenditures of money. Initiates are persuaded more and more to work long hours for the Scientologists with no payment. According to the research of James and Marcia Rudin:

> [For example,] "Sue Anne" [a former member] reports she was under constant pressure to get new members and to encourage them to spend money on auditing [courses]. . . . Most who are heavily involved in the movement live in Scientology centers or in houses or apartments with other Scientologists. . . .
> Ex-members maintain one cannot question church teachings and that authoritarian Scientology leaders keep tight discipline by paramilitary methods . . . [administered by] "Ethics Officers". . . [and] "Ethics conditions.". . . Many former Scientologists believe they were hypnotized and their thoughts controlled during

auditing. (James and Marcia Rudin, *Prison or Paradise: The New Religious Cults*, pp. 86–87)

The Rudins conclude that Scientology exhibits the basic characteristics common in religious cults, such as the Unification Church, the International Society for Krishna Consciousness, The Way International, Tony and Susan Alamo Christian Foundation, the Divine Light Mission, the Children of God, the Church of Armageddon/Love Family, and the Body of Christ. These qualities are:

1. Members swear total allegiance to an all-powerful leader whom they believe to be a messiah.

2. Rational thought or questioning is discouraged or forbidden.

3. The cult's recruitment techniques are often deceptive.

4. The cult weakens the follower psychologically and makes him believe that his problems can only be solved by the group.

5. The new cult expertly manipulates guilt, and members may be forced to "confess" their inadequacies and past "sins" before the group or certain individuals.

6. Cult members are increasingly isolated from the outside world and cut off from their pasts.

7. The cult or its leader makes every career or life decision for members.

8. Some cults promise to improve society, raise money, work for the poor, and so on. However, their energies are channeled into promoting the well-being of the group rather than improving society.

9. Cult followers often work very long hours, for little or no pay, and they are made to feel guilty or unworthy if they

protest. (James and Marcia Rudin, *Prison or Paradise: The New Religious Cults*, pp. 20–23)

Be cautious when accosted by recruiters for allegedly secular "mental health" groups or unspecified meetings. Cults may have targeted you as a vulnerable, prospective initiate.

14. What about stepping aside from organized religion and joining a humanistic cause such as Ethical Culture?

In a free society like the United States, you certainly can opt for secular humanism. Perhaps this will be a satisfactory synthesis for you in the present. However, unlike Judaism, modern secularism has not withstood the test of time. What will be your feelings toward your discarding of Jewish religion 10 or 20 or 30 years from now? An example of how a secular person's perceptions can change during the course of adulthood is Anne Roiphe's memoir entitled *Generation Without Memory*. During her young adult years, Ms. Roiphe comfortably cast aside her Judaism. "I thought of myself as tribeless, stateless, countryless, classless, religionless" (Anne Roiphe, *Generation Without Memory*, p. 80).

Later, as a married woman and a mother, this secular synthesis became less and less satisfactory. For example, when observing her daughter Becky in contrast to Becky's Jewishly identifying friend Hannah, Anne Roiphe observed:

My child has no Jewish identity. She has no non-Jewish identity. She hasn't yet heard the word [Jewish]. . . .

We have told her that we are Jewish because our parents were but that we don't go to a synagogue because we don't believe in ritual. We are humanists. . . . We are agnostics, I explained. My child has many questions [about religion] I can't answer. She is already more burdened than [her Jewish friends]. (Anne Roiphe, *Generation Without Memory*, pp. 52, 14)

More and more, Ms. Roiphe came to acknowledge her mistake in so casually casting off Judaism and Jewish identity for her family and her future offspring.

> I can see that we [Ms. Roiphe and her husband] made an error [casting Jewish traditions aside]. . . . The sense of connection to past and future that are lacking in our lives are serious losses. . . . We atone for nothing and are thankful for little. . . . We have no group cultural past and no group cultural future—this is not adequate. (Anne Roiphe, *Generation Without Memory*, p. 214)

Similarly, Letty Cottin Pogrebin's *Deborah, Golda, and Me* is an autobiographical statement by a prominent secular woman with regard to her realization later in life of the value of the Jewishness that she had disdained in her young adult years. The poignant moment of awareness for Ms. Pogrebin was the occasion of attending the *bat mitzvah* for the daughter of a friend. She was called upon to say a few words to the young honoree. Being struck by the power of this rite of passage into Jewish womanhood, Ms. Pogrebin reflected with sadness upon the lost Jewish ritual opportunities of her own daughters' childhood years.

> My daughters could not fly out to Colorado for the bat mitzvah, but I gave them my text to read. The truth is, I had written it for them as well as for Amy [the honoree]. I owed it to them. . . . My daughters have the sad distinction of having been denied by their mother what she had herself. . . .
>
> I wish I had written a sermon like this while my daughters were young enough to learn from it. I wish I had sent them to Hebrew school. I wish I had discovered my current synthesis of ritual and revisionism early enough to fuel their growing identities as Jewish women. But none of us can relive our children's childhoods. I can only hope that when they are parents, they will revert to the

[Jewish] tradition. . . . Maybe then, there will be some bar mitz-vahs and bat mitzvahs in my future. (Letty Cottin Pogrebin, *Deborah, Golda, and Me*, p. 142)

What Letty Cottin Pogrebin was reflecting at the time of Amy's *bat mitzvah* was the value of time-tested rituals for coping with life's moments of significant passage. As Rabbi Harold Kushner has written:

There are events in the lives of each of us which we don't want to have to face alone. . . . Religion [and its rituals] teaches us to face them in the company of others, our neighbors around us and our ancestors before us, who faced similar situations and left records of their experiences to enlighten and guide us. (Harold Kushner, *Who Needs God?* p. 34)

Organized religion is a critical weapon in combating existential loneliness, which is such a normal human tendency. Here again, Rabbi Kushner commands our attention.

What does religion offer that we lonely human souls need? In a word, it offers community. Our place of worship offers us a refuge [a "sanctuary"], an island of caring in the midst of a hostile, competitive world. In a society that segregates the old from the young, the rich from the poor, the successful from the struggling, the house of worship represents one place where the barriers fall and we all stand equal before God.

Can you remember a time in your life when something very good or something sad happened? Wasn't your first impulse to call someone up, to tell about it? . . . [We] needed to share it. Marriage ceremonies, funerals, and mourning customs are all ways religion gives us of taking a private event and giving it a public expression, so that we are not left alone on those emotional mountain peaks. (Harold Kushner, *Who Needs God?* pp. 103, 104–105)

How disheartening has it been for each of us when we have encountered a person who is unaffiliated, unconnected, and uncomfortable with organized religion, and who experiences a tragedy or wants to rejoice in a happy occasion. Who can they tell? With whom can they exult? Upon whom can they depend? In what fashion can they deal with the void, the emptiness of not having a ritualized routine for marking this critical passage?

15. Why doesn't the Jewish community simply solve the problem of disaffiliation by proclaiming non-Jewish spouses and children full participants in local synagogues and in Jewish life in general?

Judaism is a faith community, as is Catholicism and each of the various denominations of Protestantism. Faith communities are not simply social settings in which all fine, decent human beings can participate fully and equally. Just as certain civic privileges are available only to American citizens, so, too, are certain sacred rites of all major religions made available only to members of the faith. Relatives of faith community members should be made welcome in both synagogues and churches, but religious distinctions still remain. A non-Christian does not receive sacred "communion" rites and does not formally come to be regarded as a faith "member" of a church, even though he/she may attend services, adult education classes, social functions, and other church gatherings.

Similar principles apply to synagogues. To act otherwise is to redefine a synagogue as a social club, equally accessible to all, regardless of faith commitments and not as an American-style faith community. To involve Christian spouses and children in Jewish services, adult education lectures, family social gatherings, and so on, is praiseworthy. However, to enable practicing Christians or other non-Jews to participate as if they were Jews in Jewish ritual settings, in leadership levels within the synagogue, and so on, is to create confusion in the minds of all concerned. In addition, it blurs the critical distinction between converts and born Jews (both groups fully eligible for Jewish ritual life) and non-Jewish relatives of Jewish synagogue members. Such distinctions are increasingly advocated by Jewish policy planners, concerned about "untargeted" outreach efforts to non-Jewish family members. Dr. Rela Monson observed: "At some point we have to draw boundaries at the edge of the Jewish community in order for Jewish identity to be effectively transmitted. In the open society we have to respect the decisions of a person who chooses not to be a Jew" (Deborah Lipstadt, "The Ties That No Longer Bind," pp. 62–63). Similarly, Rabbi Steven Fuchs has pointed out: "We should encourage non-Jews (and their children) to become Jews by Choice . . . we must remind them, though, that remaining a non-Jew is also a choice, and all choices have consequences [in this case eligibility or ineligibility for faith community sacred ceremonies]" (Steven Fuchs, "Reach Out—But Also Bring In," p. 69).

16. Rabbi, isn't promoting marriage of one's own kind a view that is incompatible with our commitments to America, democracy, openness, and freedom of choice?

There are two competing visions of American culture present in the 20th century—the "melting pot" and "cultural pluralism." At the end of the 19th century and into the early years of this century, the "melting pot" doctrine sought to remake all immigrants into one white, pan-Protestant mold. Public schools of that era borrowed Protestant church architecture and sought to school the children of the newcomers into a homogeneous civic vision of a future society in which all minorities would be submerged by majority culture. This vision influenced many of the foreign-born and their offspring, and its persuasiveness has remained present down to today. It is even reflected in the assumptions upon which your question is based.

However, in contrast to "melting pot" doctrine, many social scientists offered an alternative vision, "cultural pluralism"—a mosaic of ethnic, religious, and racial communities adding to the collective strength and vitality of America precisely by authentically retaining mutually respectful differences. Today's advocates of "multiculturalism" in public education recognize the need to educate future American citizens with the awareness that the uniqueness of the United States of America throughout our history, and including the present time, has been the wealth of diversity in backgrounds, traditions, beliefs, and commitments that has characterized our political process, our cultural life, and our shared vision of "diversity within our unity." Rabbi Harold Gordon commented:

> It is the duty of men and women of different faiths, colors and nations to learn to live in peace and amity while maintaining their differences. We must learn how to live together despite differences that almost inevitably exist. It is our duty, further, to perpetuate those values and ideals that we know to be significant in our religious philosophy.
>
> Conformity is not to be mistaken for an unmixed blessing. Blandness is not virtue. The elimination of all differences in religion and color could only lead to blandness, and is, therefore, not to be mistaken for a blessing to mankind but rather as a serious threat to the welfare of individuals and the society of which they are a part. (Albert I. Gordon, *Intermarriage*, p. 368)

17. What difference does it make if—following marriage—I or my new family unit remains Jewish or becomes Christian or

some combination of both? Are not all these religions the same, simply teaching you to be a good person?

Your question opens up an important opportunity to address the misconception that many have in our day that Judaism and Christianity are indistinguishable. True, both are valid religions, but their approaches are often fundamentally at odds. At one level, Jews have a long history of suffering under persecutions that emanated from Christian teaching: deicide (the claim that the Jews killed Jesus), the Crusades, the Inquisition, the "blood libel" (the accusation that Jews needed the blood of Christian children to make *matzah* for Passover), and "the desecration of the host" (the assumption that Jews stole communion wafers and desecrated them in order to reenact the killing of Jesus). Such a legacy leaves a residual base of anti-Semitism within the Western world at large. Stemming from such age-old teachings are stubborn myths of Jews being in league with Jesus's enemy, the devil. Thus Jews as satanic forces are blamed for manipulating the economy, the media, and the political world, and Jews are held responsible for the ills of society.

At a second level, Jewish and Christian beliefs are at odds. Christianity believes that the messiah has come; Judaism claims that this has not occurred. Christian teaching assumes that God's laws as set forth in the Torah were intended to be followed in an "all or nothing" fashion, and because this was impossible to achieve, law was replaced by faith in Jesus. Jesus became the "route to salvation" (heaven) reserved for Christians alone. Everyone else was technically condemned to eternal damnation (hell). In contrast, Judaism has never viewed the law in God's Torah as "all or nothing," but rather as a comprehensive guide to living a life as a moral, ritually and spiritually fulfilled Jewish person. Faith is praiseworthy for Jews, but *mitzvot* — positive actions, doing God's commandments — are the sole vehicle for achieving God's favor, and good deeds are open to all of mankind.

Third, Jewish and Christian ceremonies are incompatible. Rabbi Harold Schulweis has written that the Eucharist (wafer used in Christian communion which represents the body of Jesus) is not Passover *matzah*. Baptism (cleansing the newborn baby of his/her "trace" of Adam and Eve's "original sin") is not the Jewish *bris* (covenant of circumcision). The Christian "Old Testament" (which retranslates words to "harmonize" prophecy with the subsequent life of Jesus, and rearranges books to imply the end of Judaism and the victory of Jesus' followers) is not the Jewish Bible (Harold Schulweis, "The Hyphen Between the Cross and the Star," pp. 171–173). Rabbi Schulweis concludes:

> [Prospective interfaith couples like] Peggy and Sam may have to come to understand that true tolerance does not entail wholesale adoption of all faiths, and that openness does not mean reducing all traditions to sameness. . . . Their resolve to hold clashing traditions in one household not only distorts the uniqueness of each faith civilization, but compromises their own integrity. . . . Judaism and Christianity are particular languages, with their own precious syntaxes, which when thrown together, produce a babble of tongues. (Harold Schulweis, "The Hyphen Between the Cross and the Star," p. 176)

Choosing a religion is a serious matter. It affects many sacred moments of one's lifetime. Neither Christianity nor Judaism is well served by trivializing the real and fundamental differences that separate these two mutually respectful yet distinct approaches to God, to spirituality, and to religious value systems. Be aware that marrying into a Christian family may mean acquiring relatives who believe in the charge of deicide, who accept the idea that the souls of all non-Christians are damned, and so on.

Each religion is unique, distinctive, and, by definition, incompatible with any other. Mutual respect for differences is praiseworthy in religious affairs; syncretism (the blending of two contradictory, irreconcilable faiths) is both confusing and dishonest! Since the two faiths so often stand in contradiction to one another, it is demeaning to both traditions to pretend that they can authentically coexist in the same household! (See Appendix I for more information on the distinctions between Judaism and Christianity.)

18. Rabbi, why do Christian clergy—ministers and priests—seem less concerned about intermarriage than our Jewish leaders?

Several reasons should be shared in this regard. First, the vast majority of Americans are Christian. Since Christianity is therefore, by far, the majority religion in American life, its survival is not imperiled. To Christian leaders, intermarriage with Jews is simply a numerically insignificant "ripple" in the sea of Christendom. Of much greater numerical and substantive dismay to priests and ministers in America is the spread of secularism, of opting to be "nothing." However, in Israel, where Christians represent a tiny minority, great vigilance is accorded to the preservation of Christian neighborhoods, Christian local autonomy, and the transmission of Christian identity to the next generation, lest they be swallowed over time by the vast "sea" of Israeli Jews and Moslems. In other words, where they are tiny minorities, both Christian and Jewish clergy fear disappearance. In majority settings, each one's concern is greatly diminished.

Second, unlike Judaism, Christianity is not premised upon being the religion of a religiously unified family, community, and "chain of tradition." Instead, it is the religion of the individual. Frequently, American Christian families have had a Catholic mother married to a Methodist father, with children active in the Presbyterian church. Many Christians switch from one denomination to another as a personal "faith" commitment. The affiliation of each individual is what counts, rather than that of the family unit. Synagogues count their membership on the basis of a certain number of "family members." Churches list individuals.

Third, not all Christian clergy are comfortable with intermarriage between Christians and Jews. In general, the more liberal groups are comfortable, whereas more traditionally minded Evangelicals are visibly troubled by this trend. Tens of millions of American born-again Christians firmly believe that only passionately baptized and believing Christians will achieve "salvation" in the "hereafter," and they are opposed to adding "unredeemed" persons to their family structure. In other words, Christianity, like Judaism, has a wide spectrum of responses. Finally, whereas Judaism sees Christianity as incompatible with Jewish views of the messiah, of the afterlife, of chosenness, and so on, liberal Christian clergy who accept intermarriage are comforted by a belief that Judaism is not only compatible with Christianity, but represents its roots, its heritage.

Consequently, for all of the above reasons, it is not surprising that Christian clergy have a different view of intermarriage. Yet Rabbi Albert Gordon has written:

> Jewish, Catholic and Protestant religious groups wish to survive not only because the desire for life is characteristic of normal, healthy people and groups, but because each religion believes that the elimination of the values by which it lives would be a disservice to the total society of which it is a part. It believes further that its unique "way" represents the path that God has directed man to take. Identification with the group then is tantamount to identification with its values as well. However much one may argue about the real worth of these values, the fact remains that to each group they have significance, and no religious group will willingly give them up. (Albert I. Gordon, *Intermarriage*, p. 366)

In a society that is overwhelmingly Christian, Christian clergy can afford to be ambivalent about mixed marriage. Time is on their side. The long-term, multigenerational impact of mixed marriage means disintegration for the minority religious groups. For Judaism, a minority religion threatened with assimilation, a religion of the entire family unit, a religion manifested most prominently in its traditions, and a faith viewed as incompatible with Christianity, intermarriage involves serious grounds for concern.

19. Perhaps all of this is true. But if so, what difference should it make to me? Why be Jewish at all?

The question "Why Be Jewish?" in an age of choices is critical for our discussion. Today in an open society, we can choose our state of residence, our career, our hair color, the shape of our physical features. Even sex-change operations are possible. So why not be free to choose a different religion? What difference does it make if we remain Jewish or not? Several critical reasons come to mind.

First, we owe it to God. We Jews have had more than 3,000 years of an unbroken chain of tradition, a covenantal bond to represent ethical monotheism in this world. Three thousand years represent at least 150 generations of bringing to humankind the message that God and God alone is to be worshiped; His message is that all human beings must be moral in their behavior toward one another and toward the universe as well. We owe it to God to remain Jewish and to keep Judaism alive.

Second, we owe it to our ancestors. They kept alive the unbroken chain of tradition, sometimes at great peril to their lives, in order to pass this precious legacy on to the next generation, and ultimately on to us. Some of our ancestors may have been pious and others secular, but each link in the chain recognized that unless they passed the baton on to the next in line, they would deny their sons and daughters and grandchildren the opportunity to choose whether or not to be intimately involved in the riches of Jewish ritual, values, learning, wisdom, and spirituality. We owe it to our ancestors and to our descendants not to be the end of that millennia-long chain of transmission.

Third, we owe it to our fellow Jews of today. As was demonstrated by the tragedies of the Holocaust and by the euphoria of the creation of the modern State of Israel, in a modern age of technologies of genocide and mass destruction, more than ever individual Jews in distress rely upon one another for support, for help, for rescue. Unique among the peoples of the world, Jewry sustained the morale of Jews behind the Iron Curtain of the U.S.S.R. and is bringing unprecedented hundreds of thousands into freedom. In unmatched acts of bravery, while other civilizations witnessed the deaths of thousands of Ethiopians of all religions due to famine, civil war, and lawlessness, Jewry alone rescued tens of thousands of Ethiopian Jews, by plane, by ship, by bribe, by whatever was necessary to save the lives of our people. And in unparalleled outpourings of philanthropy, world Jewry has consistently aided the unequaled struggle for survival and for the absorption of diverse immigrants occurring over the past four decades within Israeli society. We owe it to our fellow Jews to remain Jewish.

Fourth, we owe it to the world. Judaism and the Jewish people have made profound contributions to world culture, science, and ethics, far in excess of our tiny numbers and dispersion. Prominent persons of Jewish heritage have been as diverse as Karl Marx, Sigmund Freud, Albert Einstein, Louis Brandeis, Jonas Salk, Maimonides, Saul of Tarsus (Jesus's primary disciple), and even some of the sailors who arrived with Columbus on his maiden voyage to North America. Our religious imperative for learning, for scientific inquiry, for improving upon God's world, for creating a moral society has set the groundwork for ongoing profound Jewish contributions to virtually every sector of societal evolution. We owe it to the world to remain Jewish.

Finally, we owe it to ourselves to remain Jewish. Judaism is a fantastic religious approach to every facet of our lives. Sincere converts to Judaism are quick to point out the blessings of Judaism, the contrast of our religion to others around us. Judaism offers a meaningful process for dealing with mourning the loss of loved ones, a celebratory formula for rejoicing at birth, a passionate sanctification of marriage. Judaism provides a rich medley of holidays, with emotions ranging from the serious introspection of Yom Kippur to the hilarity of Purim, to the hospitality of Passover. Judaism offers a legacy of learning, of questioning, of freedom to find a range of permitted answers to vexing contemporary moral problems. Paraphrasing the caution offered by Dennis Prager and Joseph Telushkin: Do not discard a priceless heirloom of Jewish heritage that you may hardly know:

> You may be able to judge the Judaism of your parents and/or the Judaism of your local temple; but the Judaism which has survived 3,500 years, the Judaism which bequeathed to the world God and universal morality, the Judaism which survived Pharaoh, Rome, the Crusades . . . Hitler and Stalin, and the Judaism which today puts the Jewish people at the vortex of human affairs, is the authentic and powerful Judaism of which sadly, you [might] know very little. (Dennis Prager and Joseph Telushkin, *Nine Questions People Ask About Judaism*, p. 139)

Before you discard this incredible heritage, study it, savor it. (See chapter 5 for a full discussion of "Why Be Jewish.") It will enrich your life. We owe it to ourselves to remain Jewish.

20. Isn't all of this discussion futile? In our open society, with a reported 50 percent intermarriage rate growing at a rapid pace, is not interfaith marriage inevitable?

The recent data as reported by the national news media is quite misleading. The 50-plus percent intermarriage rate should be broken down into two separate groups. The first group, adult children of earlier mixed-married households, as expected, is intermarrying at a rate that approaches 90 percent. As discussed earlier, the retention of such young men and women in the Jewish fold is statistically unlikely. However, of the second group, the adult offspring of two Jewish parents, the intermarriage rate is considerably lower. It is high, to be sure, but not dramatically higher than 10 or 15 years ago. The growth of this figure is related to the sizable increase in the intermarrying rate for young Jewish women who, in contrast to past generations, routinely live away at college and graduate school and venture into the wide range of occupations previously limited to Jewish males. Whereas Jewish men used to marry non-Jews much more frequently than did Jewish women, this disparity is no longer the case today.

Yet even this figure of less than 50 percent is misleading. It contains the high intermarrying percentage among sons and daughters of two-Jewish-parent households who are unaffiliated with any synagogue or religious movement. It is also distorted, within a national survey, by the near universal intermarriage rate in small Jewish communities within America's vast hinterland. Thus, in densely populated Jewish areas in which large clusters of Jews reside, the intermarriage rate among adult offspring of synagogue-affiliated families with two Jewish parents is considerably less than the rate reported by the national survey. Although such a number is not without peril to Jewish survival, we should not assume that intermarriage among committed American Jewish families is rampant and totally out of control. Instead, we should provide ever more encouragement to those who are marrying within the community. What we say and do to encourage in-marriage does make a difference. We should not consider ourselves powerless.

Ruby Jo Kennedy wrote in her classic essay "Single or Triple Melting Pot?": "Intermarriage does not relentlessly increase in the dimension of time in a smooth, unbroken pattern. . . . No mystical force pushes any aspect of intergroup relations in a single pattern" (Ruby Jo Kennedy, "Single or Triple Melting Pot? Intermarriage Trends in New Haven, 1870–1940," p. 333; also Albert I. Gordon, *Intermarriage*, p. 367).

In the 1960s no one would have predicted the remarkable resurgence of Orthodox Judaism within American life and its growth in America's affluent suburbs. Nor would anyone have guessed that Jewish day school enrollment would grow from trivial numbers three decades ago to its current enrollment of more than 30 percent of all Jewish children in the United States receiving some type of Jewish education. Today, no one should be bold enough to prophecy what the future has in store with regard to American Jewish marital patterns. If we act forcefully to introduce single Jews to one another, if this is a budgeted priority in Jewish communities, and if we are willing to actively advocate in-marriage, out-marriage need not be inevitable!

21. Rabbi, if you are so concerned about the implications of intermarriage, why are you willing to spend so much time working with prospective converts and mixed-marrieds grappling with Judaism?

People like myself who are passionately devoted to the survival of Judaism are anxious to respond to intermarriage in an active fashion suitable to each situation. Once intermarriage has occurred, we must do whatever is possible to facilitate the unifying of the existing family unit as a Jewish family via the route of sincere, meaningful conversion. Thus I train numerous conversionary families in Judaism each year, providing extensive instruction as well as opportunities for growing levels of observance.

If conversion is not contemplated for the non-Jewish family members, I am committed to offering maximum encouragement for the Jewish family members to increase their level of knowledge and participation in Jewish ritual and practice and to raise their offspring as Jews. Once intermarriage is a fact, conversion and outreach are priority concerns.

It is precisely the intensity of my work with the intermarried that fuels my passion for simultaneously promoting *endogamy* (in-marriage) among Jews. Involvement in conversion and outreach makes one acutely aware of how few mixed-married couples opt for such Judaizing of their lives and how complex the endeavor is for many who do choose the Jewish option. There is an obvious corollary for such a common painful reality. It is the need to educate Jewish single persons interested in preserving their own present and future connection with Jewish tradition. In-marriage is vital to Jewish survival. If Jews truly want to assure the continuity of Judaism, they should seek to marry fellow Jews.

Rabbi Jacob Philip Rudin authored the following letter in 1970 to "an angry student" offended that Rabbi Rudin would not agree to officiate at his intermarriage wedding ceremony. The rabbi stressed:

Nothing which I have written has been said in any derogatory spirit. I respect non-Jews, just as I want them to respect me. I want them to have the rights of freedom of belief, of conscience and worship, just as I want those freedoms for myself. I don't consider Judaism superior to another faith. I am only saying that Judaism is my faith, Jewish destiny is my destiny, and I want my faith and my destiny to live and to flourish.

I know that only Jews will keep Judaism alive. I cannot expect non-Jews to do so. It needs a Jewish home, Jewish observance, two Jewish parents, the synagogue as the family's only sanctuary and not a half-sanctuary. It needs concern, deep, abiding, compassionate, for the Jewish people and not merely a generalized humanitarian interest in people. (Jacob Philip Rudin, *A Harvest of Forty Years in the Pulpit*, p. 168)

Jewish survival, the continued covenantal relationship of Jews with God, will be assured if, and only if, such Jewish familial commitments are maintained. Sincere, committed converts are always welcome but are statistically rare. Involved Jewish children of the mixed-married are to be encouraged but are sadly a minority in numbers. *Intermarriage is not an "opportunity" for Jewish growth; it is a potential peril to Jewish survival!* The clearest, most promising route toward preserving the precious legacy of Judaism is *endogamy,* Jewish people of all ages marrying one another. Anything else leaves those of us committed to Jewish life laden with grounds for concern.

2

Interdating and Intermarriage: A Jewish Parents' Guide

M any parents look forward to their children's futures with anxiety, fearing that their children will not choose Jewish mates. Yet many of these parents are reluctant to articulate their concerns because they do not know how to broach the emotional subjects of interdating and intermarriage. Although they have powerful implications for their family's future, these subjects can be extremely awkward. They may challenge the parents' commitment to Jewish identity and may force the family to confront its acceptance of intermarried couples within the extended family.

This chapter addresses parents' concerns as well as their fears and insecurities in order to encourage them to speak with their children on the perils of interdating and intermarriage.

1. How would my child's intermarrying pose a risk to Jewish survival?

On the basis of the 1990 National Jewish Population Survey, several points should be made clear both to you and to your offspring. First, although many Jews by Choice become wonderful additions to the Jewish community, in more than 95 percent of intermarriages the Gentile partner does not convert to Judaism. Second, even though some interfaith families do raise their children as Jews, 72 percent of the children of the intermarried identify as other than Jewish. At least half of the remaining 28 percent of these youngsters are only nominally "Jewish" (i.e., no religious school education, synagogue affiliation, or *bar/bat mitzvah*, etc). The statistical likelihood of young children reared in such households growing into adulthood identifying with the Jewish religion, marrying Jews, setting up Jewish homes, and raising Jewish children is infinitesimally tiny.

Furthermore, keep in mind that if you remain silent, your inaction is also a response. Silence will be interpreted by your youngsters as indicative of your approval. If the Jewishness of your descendants is important to you, then take seriously the implications to Jewish survival posed by interdating and intermarriage. You should consistently and rationally verbalize your concerns!

2. My children will never share my point of view. Why bother to engage them in a conversation about interdating/intermarriage? It is a waste of time, an exercise in futility.

Many well-intentioned parents confuse a frank and clear articulation of their values with seeking to win an argument. It is unlikely that your teenager will calmly listen to your point of view, and then admit: "Mom, you are right. You have shown me the error of my ways." Such a fairy-tale ending is unlikely when discussing any topic, let alone a subject fraught with such potentially passionate disagreements. Nevertheless, the absence of immediate "victory" should not be mistaken for failure. A parent has gained by imparting clear-cut answers to the next generation. That is the meaning of the phrase in the *Sh'ma*, "You shall teach [articulate] them [Jewish values] diligently to your children [of all ages]" (Deuteronomy 6:9). Parents are not commanded to win arguments, but rather to plant the kernels of Jewish ideas. God willing, the "seeding" process will reach fruition at a later date.

Conversely, without the transmission of values, the secularism of society at large will likely replace Jewish priorities. As many family psychologists recommend to parents:

> Communicate your values without apology—and expect them to be challenged. Teenagers [and young adults] are trying to find out who and what they are. They are also trying to separate from us. They *want* to be independent from us and have their own identities. We want that, too! Sometimes they will do or say outlandish things to show us they are individuals. When this acting-out involves sex and sexuality [and/or interdating, intermarriage], we must continue to say what we believe. . . . We're going to be told we're old-fashioned or out of it. All teenagers [and young adults] do that to their parents—and we probably did it to our own, at least behind their backs. We should not take it personally. (Andrea Warren and Jay Wiedenkeller, *Everybody's Doing It: How to Survive Your Teenagers' Sex Life (and Help Them Survive It, Too)*, p. 217)

During the early 1960s, a very independent-minded and articulate cousin of mine consistently debated Jewish mores with her parents. As a younger bystander, I don't remember these marathon ideological exchanges ever ending with "surrender" by either side. Nevertheless, my aunt and uncle verbalized clear and consistent positions. During my cousin's senior year of high school, she wrote a "Dear Abby" column for the school newspaper. Her answers invariably drew upon the well-reasoned and comprehensive value system that had been spelled out in great detail during the earlier debates with her parents, proof that the long-term transmission of values had registered with her. Furthermore, as a devoted parent today, it is clear that her strong Jewish commitments are indebted to the concrete formulation of Jewishness present within her childhood household.

Although challenging the value-free norms of the outside world with which our children test our limits is both unpleasant and frequently confrontational, we must persist in this parenting responsibility. Research has verified the platitude that parental seriousness in regard to Jewish dating, marriage, and child-rearing practices can have a substantial impact. Recently, a 31-year-old acquaintance, in advance of his wedding, acknowledged:

> My fiancee is the first Jewish girl I have ever had a serious relationship with. I have come to realize that everything my parents have been telling me about how much easier life would be with a Jewish girl is true. But even more importantly, how much more our relationship has been enhanced by growing up with the same traditions, values, morals and beliefs. Together as a couple we will shape our destiny with many of these tenets and traditions at its foundation. . . . [This past High Holy Day season] as we fasted, went to temple, or even made matzah-ball soup, a lot of this stuff started making sense to me. (Finally!) (Louis Shuckman, letter to Rabbi Alan Silverstein, September 5, 1993)

Not surprisingly, in households in which parental indifference greets interdating/intermarriage, the behavior of sons and daughters regarding Jewish survival is predictably apathetic. Nearly 75 percent of Jewish adults brought up in homes in which parents failed to join a synagogue intermarry. In contrast, affiliated households in which concerns about interdating and intermarriage are expressed experience a rate of out-marriage of less than 20 percent. Furthermore, when parental concerns have been consistently expressed, the chances of the non-Jewish partner considering conversion to Judaism are much greater. Rabbis Mark Winer and Aryeh Meir have written:

> Children generally respect [whether they admit it or not] parental authority that is consistent, rational. . . . Studies of Jewish college students found that there was less likelihood of intermarriage where parents were very clear and consistent with their children in voicing their opposition. . . . While there is no guarantee that our children will marry Jews, we improve the odds by sending a clear and unambiguous message of what we expect and why. (Mark Winer and Aryeh Meir, original draft of *Questions Jewish Parents Ask About Intermarriage: A Guide for Jewish Families*, p. 16)

The expression of parental concerns about interdating/intermarriage does make a difference. It should be voiced often. It is worth the extra effort!

3. Might I be impairing my relationship with my child if he/she gets angry at my "intrusion" into his/her dating or marital plans?

Do not refrain from honest exchanges with your son or daughter about any subject that is fundamental to your value system. Do not confuse disagreements with your offspring with *removal of love* from them. Psychiatrist Tom Rusk has written: "Barriers to human communication [include] . . . [the] difficulty [everyone has in] handling strong feelings. . . . Feelings are facts to the person experiencing them. . . . We rarely discuss issues of power openly. . . . We tend to react with blame and self-defense" (Tom Rusk and Patrick D. Miller, *The Power of Ethical Persuasion*, p. iii).Yet a true relationship between parents and offspring of any age must include an ongoing exchange of basic beliefs and principled points of view. Dialogues regarding values need not involve shouting or threats of punishment, but rather must impart necessary information on both sides. Dr. Rusk cautions: "Problem-solving can wait until full mutual understanding is achieved." However, without the transmission of a Jewish referent from parents, children are unlikely to hear anything but the popular, assimilationist messages of television and movies, the campus and business worlds. Just as parents express opinions about the necessity of their children achieving admirable grades in school, entering an appropriate college, choosing a viable career, and not resorting to alcohol or drugs, so too must they express themselves about dating and marriage. While our sons and daughters might protest that it is their lives, not ours, at some deeper level they realize that their choice of college, job, potential addictions, and spouse will have an impact upon parents as well. In any of these serious arenas, you cannot allow yourselves to be reduced to passive bystanders or impartial observers.

Only one generation ago young people generally avoided interdating/intermarriage on the strength of parental beliefs and statements. Now, many teens and young adults sense their parents' awkwardness at addressing these topics as a license to experiment. It is essential that parents not wait until it is too late to articulate their point of view.

4. How can I justify my views about Judaism when my children see that I am not observant? Wouldn't I be hypocritical?

It is true that a consistent involvement in Jewish ritual and synagogue attendance provide a parent with a natural framework to justify advocacy of in-marriage. It is never too late to adopt such commitments, which will have a cumulative effect upon a household, building memories, shaping Judaism's relevance in people's lives. Yet, if you are still not observant, it does not mean that your genuine concern for preserving the

blessings and joys of Judaism within your family is hypocritical. Do not allow this false logic to intimidate you. Commitment to Judaism manifests itself in many nonreligious ways as
well.

Do you care about the fate of the State of Israel and the
Jewish people worldwide? Are you distressed when anti-
Semitic acts occur? Are you proud of the incredible number of
Jews who have received Nobel Prizes and in other ways have
contributed to society? Do you value Judaism's age-old em-
phasis upon learning, questioning, searching for truth? Do
you appreciate the unique response of Jews when coreligionists are in trouble, either abroad or at home? Do you cherish
being a link in a chain of Jewish tradition that spans more than
150 generations and several millennia? Do you have high regard for Jewish family values and closeness? Does the memory
of the Holocaust pierce the inner being of your soul? Have you
felt the spiritual and psychological/emotional value of Jewish
ritual when coping with transitional moments in your life,
such as at birth (*brit milah*, baby-naming), adolescence (*bar/bat
mitzvah*), marriage (*huppah* ceremony), and death (Jewish funeral, burial, and *shivah*)? Have you been especially moved
while in a Jewish setting, when watching your grandmother
light holiday candles, when praying for recovery from an illness, when seeking solace when a loved one died, when
rejoicing at the birth of a child? If you answered any, many, or
all of these questions in the affirmative, then Judaism and its
transmission to the next generation mean a great deal to you.
Professor Arnold Eisen of Stanford has commented:

> American Jews are more Jewish than they themselves real-
> ize. . . . The Jewishness of American Jews lies in all sorts of
> unexpected places. . . . [For example] a person's profession can
> also be a source of Jewish meaning. Several years ago . . . Jewish
> doctors across the United States founded the Maimonides Soci-
> ety, which is thriving because . . . [many] Jewish doctors are not

coincidentally Jewish and physicians; Jewishness is wrapped up in their professional life. Friendship, family, public activity and politics are sources of Jewish meaning [for many Jewish people]. (Arnold Eisen, "The Role of a Jewish Research Institute," p. 8)

There is a lot more God out there in people than we are often given credit for. I find that when I speak in the American Jewish community . . . [in] largely secular segments of the American Jewish community, people are having experiences of God, not every day, but in their lives they are having them. (Arnold Eisen, "Abraham Joshua Heschel," audiotape)

The fact that you, too, have some of these feelings and associations should empower you to articulate your concerns about interdating and intermarriage.

I recall my own family's experiences. Neither of my two grandfathers was religiously observant. Early in 20th-century America, Jewish immigrants struggled seven days a week to support their families. There was no time for leisure or for religious devotion. Yet both of my grandfathers passionately valued being Jewish. They recognized that they were part of an age-old process of transmitting the precious legacy of Judaism from one generation to the next. In some generations, members of my family were religiously observant. At other moments, my ancestors were primarily involved in Jewish self-help societies, or still others were concerned with Jewish learning. Regardless of their levels of observance, each generation articulated its opposition to intermarriage. They did their utmost to fulfill the responsibility of passing the banner of Judaism on to their successors so that the newest members of the family would be able to make their own positive choices about the nature of their Jewish involvements. It is due to my two grandfathers that, in the 1990s, both my sister and I are privileged to be raising children as religiously observant youngsters, a gift made possible by seemingly irreligious predecessors.

Do not underestimate the crucial role parents play in making the "smorgasbord" of Jewish identity, involvements, and enhancements available to your children and future grandchildren.

> Traditionally, Jews "absorbed" their Jewish education by being immersed in an organic Jewish culture . . . [consisting of] their family life, the schools they attended, and the communities of which they were a part. . . . [The family remains] the most important influence in shaping children's basic Jewish identity and attitudes. (Bernard Reisman, "Informal Jewish Education in North America," p. 32)

Jewish family experiences are critical to the future Jewish perspectives of your offspring. Thus, if you are observant, make sure to involve your children in both home and synagogue practices. If you are a reader of Jewish books or a connoisseur of Jewish films and Jewish current issues, articulate your interests to your children. If your commitment is in the realm of Jewish communal life through the federations and United Jewish Appeal (UJA), the American Jewish Committee, ORT, the National Council of Jewish Women, and so on, make a point of discussing your activities. If your involvement is in synagogue, Men's Club, or Sisterhood, explain why you devote this time and effort. If you contribute *tzedakah* to Israel, to domestic Jewish concerns, or to Jewish groups aiding society at large, make your moral investments known. If you are an activist on behalf of new immigrants, the homeless, the hungry, downtrodden, ill or isolated, this too should be expressed in concrete terms to the next generation.

Rabbi Jack Moline teaches in his forthcoming book, *10 Things Parents Should Say More Often to Their Children*, that it is essential to share with your nuclear family your personal feelings about God, about the commitments Jews make to assist one another, about the value of Judaism for enriching your family life, and so on. Whether or not you are religiously observant, you care a great deal about Judaism. Jewish transmission rests squarely in your hands.

5. How can I reconcile concerns about interdating/intermarriage with my desire for a full involvement in American society and an openness to friendships with non-Jews?

America is a great blessing for Jews. However, American culture includes many often-contradictory trends. For example, when people point to the American "melting pot" of one language, one set of civic assumptions, they often forget that America has always stood for cultural pluralism, the retention of distinctive religious, ethnic, and national customs, values, and points of view. America is really a harmonious orchestra with constituent groups, each playing one's own authentic instruments. More and more, civic leaders speak of the American mosaic of multiculturalism, of preserving the diversity of its citizenry.

Furthermore, while it is true that America does offer the opportunity to assimilate, this usually refers to abandoning organized religion, to becoming secularized, to being "unchurched." In reality, most Americans do not choose this extreme option. Instead, the rates of church/synagogue membership have been in constant ascent throughout American history: 7 percent in 1776; 37 percent by 1850; 50 percent by 1930; 62 percent by 1980. While Americans are free to cast religion aside, in actuality the percentage who express a belief in God has climbed to a record high of 96-plus percent, a level that exceeds virtually every other country in the world. Moreover, Americans have achieved unprecedented levels of church/synagogue-based voluntarism and charitable giving. Harold Bloom concluded in *The American Religion*, "America is a religion-mad country. It has been inflamed in this regard for about two centuries now" (cited in Martha Fay, *Do Children Need Religion?* p. xvi).

Researcher Martha Fay noted in her investigations among unchurched parents: "Naming oneself religiously, and naming one's children, seems to be a particular necessity in America. It is hard to get away from it, even if one tries" (Martha Fay, *Do Children Need Religion?* p. 201).

Thus, to be an American does not necessarily mean either to abandon one's background or to discard religious affiliation and beliefs. Instead, it is precisely the freedom of religious groups to compete within America's "free marketplace of souls" that has added to the unique vitality of both American Judaism and American Christianity. Since the mid-1980s, the pendulum of American societal behavior has been swinging noticeably toward increasing piety rather than toward the relative nonaffiliation of the 1970s. In American synagogue life, there are now more children being sent to Jewish day schools than ever before, more young adults attending Saturday morning services on a regular basis, more Jews contributing to UJA/Federation campaigns, traveling to Israel, enrolling in Judaic studies on campus, and so on. To be an advocate of Jewish continuity, Jewish dating/marriage, survival, and vitality does not put you out of sync with American trends.

Additionally, encouraging your sons and daughters to have non-Jewish friends is not at all inconsistent with expressing genuine concerns about interdating/intermarriage. For many decades, American Judaism has maintained the difference between the fellowship of close friendships and the one-to-one intimacy of dating. Many American Jews grew up in small towns cultivating lifelong bonds with Christian friends, yet scrupulously limited dating to Jews. Similarly, I have officiated at many weddings in which a Jewish bride and groom have encouraged Gentile friends to be witnesses to the civil license, to be ushers, best man, or maid of honor. These were all recognitions of a close camaraderie that did not involve either dating or intermarriage.

With these clarifications of being good Americans and of socializing with everyone, yet dating/marrying only Jews, Rabbi Sanford Seltzer has noted: "If . . . [Jewish families are] serious about stemming the tide of intermarriage, the permissive attitudes of . . . Jewish parents regarding the dating patterns of their children should no longer be ignored" (cited in Mark L. Winer, "Mom, We're Just Dating," p. 229).

6. When so many other Jewishly identifying parents take no stand whatsoever against interdating/intermarriage, how can I set myself apart?

Once again, the issue of good parenting must be separated from peer pressure. You would never tolerate destructive choices by your child in terms of drugs, alcoholism, or dropping out of school, even if other parents were indifferent. Let's be honest. Whenever any of us feels strongly or passionately, we make our opinions known to our children whether or not other mothers and fathers are equally sensitive to the issues. If interdating/intermarriage is going to make you unique in the neighborhood, so be it. It is worth the notoriety. It may not represent a perfect solution to the problem of Jewish continuity, but it does indicate your fulfillment of fundamental Jewish parental responsibilities.

The conclusions of the most recent sociological studies of intermarried couples conclude that "those [parents] who exhibit the most permissive attitudes toward their children interdating are most likely to have children who have married non-Jews" (Mark Winer, "Mom, We're Just Dating," p. 229). The appeasement strategy of permissive Jewish parents may bring momentary tranquillity; however, if they care about a Jewish future, these mothers and fathers face much greater personal anguish. They may eventually have grandchildren who will not be Jewish and may realize too late that they had not done their utmost to prevent it.

7. How can I oppose interdating/intermarriage when I accept intermarried members of our extended family?

There is a difference between what is expected in advance and coping with unapproved behavior after the fact. In spite of admonishments by parents and friends, a relative may have interdated and intermarried. After the fact, parents should not abandon members of the extended family. Nevertheless, efforts to cope with these departures from family norms should not be confused with parental approval.

Moreover, by the time they are teenagers, children are aware of the different ways in which we treat the behavior of other family units that are part of our extended family. If a sister and brother-in-law choose to live in Asia, far away from family members, you still love them, but your own sons and daughters know that your household's value system is different. The same is true if your first cousin's family become Buddhists, or if they choose to fill their home with four dogs, five cats, three birds, and a host of other pets. Children understand that all nuclear families do not act in identical fashion, even though we love and appreciate them.

So, too, when siblings, cousins, or parents intermarry, we do not cut off affection for them, but we do not have to adopt their ways of life. In the words of Rabbi Janet Marder, "It is not enough to be [a family which exhibits] . . . acceptance and accommodation [of intermarried relatives]. We must also [display as nuclear families] . . . Jewish affirmation and assertiveness [to preserving Judaism within our own homes]" ("New Perspectives on Reform Jewish Outreach," p. 7). The fact that close relations have not married other Jews should not dissuade us from advocating in-marriage and opposing interdating, any more than our Jewish priorities will dampen the ardor non-Jewish relatives might have for raising their offspring as committed Christians.

8. What are some of the blessings and joys of being Jewish, having Jewish descendants, being part of the Jewish chain of tradition?

Being Jewish is being part of a tremendously fulfilling heritage. It is special to each of us in different ways. For cerebral types, Judaism is an intellectual delight, offering a smorgasbord of great books, a love of learning, inspiring values, compelling ideas, passionate ideologies. It is open to constant questioning. Is it any wonder that Jewish life has produced an extraordinary number of Nobel prize winners, scholars, writers, inventors, researchers, philosophers, social critics?

For "hands-on Jews," Judaism offers an infinite variety of projects to better the world, both for our fellow Jews and universally. Jewish agencies such as boards of Jewish education, Jewish family services, Jewish vocational services, Jewish community centers, Jewish senior citizens homes and centers, Jewish immigrant absorption programs, and the UJA are the envy of all of American religious communities.

For spiritually oriented Jews, Judaism provides an array of rituals, life-cycle ceremonies, holidays, prayers, and symbols that have withstood the tests of time and dispersion. Judaism is a path toward holiness, an encounter with God's presence in this world, giving cosmic sense to our lives. Moreover, after several millennia of sacred survival, we owe it to God, to our ancestors, to fellow Jews, and to the world, which benefits by Judaism's ongoing contributions to remain Jews and to pass our legacy on to future generations!

9. Beyond dialogue, what actions can I take to diminish the likelihood of my children intermarrying?

HIGH-SCHOOL YEARS

In most cases, intermarriage is more a product of chance than of ideology. People marry the people whom they meet. The individuals whom our sons and daughters are most likely to choose as adult friends are persons with qualities similar to those of their early dating partners. Consequently, it is critical to structure adolescent and young adult situations in which Jewish friendships and networking are cultivated. For these reasons, parents should aggressively promote their children's involvement in post-*bar/bat mitzvah* Jewish social and educational settings.

This is the hidden benefit, for example, of attending a Hebrew school or Jewish day school at the high-school level. These educational settings build upon the base of pre-*bar/bat mitzvah* knowledge and forge a pattern of Jewish socialization. Whereas pre-*bar/bat* mitzvah Hebrew school may be compulsory, youngsters must *choose* to continue to learn about the relevance of the Jewish heritage to their lives as modern Jews and must *select* whether to be in the company of other Jewish teens on a regular basis. The 1990 National Jewish Population Survey revealed the following analysis of educational factors:

> American Jewish adults under age 45 who received . . . more than six years [ages 8–13] of [Jewish] supplementary school or day school—are more likely . . . to be married to a Jew, to prefer living in a Jewish neighborhood, to join and attend synagogue and to perform Jewish rituals [as well as virtually every other indicator of Jewish identity]. (Barry A. Kosmin et al., *Highlights of the CJF 1990 National Jewish Population Survey*, p. 31)

Thus, if we allow 13-year-olds to "drop out" of a Jewish pattern of living, we are beginning the pattern of terminal distancing from Jewish peers and commitments.

Equally important, and especially for youngsters not attending Hebrew high school, is membership in a Jewish youth group, such as United Synagogue Youth (USY), Young Judea, B'nai B'rith Youth, and JCC clubs. The best choice, if possible, is your congregation's Kadimah and USY chapters, which offer a network of youngsters from similar affiliations at the regional and national level. They provide a natural framework for synagogue follow-up and reinforcement. Moreover, USY and Kadimah build an identity with your religious movement, planting seeds of future membership with a Conservative congregation during adult years.

However, card-carrying affiliation in a youth group is not enough. Parents need to encourage—however they can—regular attendance at chapter activities, supplemented by weekend *Shabbaton* experiences and week-long encampments. This is the ideal opportunity to meet Jewish teens from other communities and to feel part of a larger network of Jewish youth. Being part of a totally Jewish communal environment, even for a few days, can "intensify the youngsters' Jewish feelings, strengthen their Jewish convictions, and provide them with peer-group support" (Hayim Halevy Donin, *To Raise a Jewish Child*, p. 108).

Whenever possible, parents should also send their children to Jewish summer camps and encourage ongoing relationships with camp friends during the school year. Jewish camps such as the JCC Camps, Tel Yehuda, and Conservative Judaism's Camps Ramah (which maximize the supplementary benefits of movement identification and networking) "create a Jewish atmosphere, impart Jewish knowledge, motivate commitment to a Jewish way of life, and demonstrate the relevance of Judaism to daily living" (Hayim Halevy Donin, *To Raise a Jewish Child*, p. 101). Camp buddies often become lifelong friends and are particularly important during college and single years. Perhaps nonsectarian camps have better waterskiing, mountain climbing, or exotic adventures, but only Jewish camps provide the types of experiences necessary for promoting Jewish identity.

Parents ought to supplement these efforts with trips to Israel as part of Jewish teen travel programs, ideally through Summer USY Pilgrimage or Ramah Seminar, USY High School in Israel (8 weeks of study for high school credit), or comparable trips. Surveys show that the prospect of inmarriage is significantly improved for young adults who spend meaningful time in Israel.

> The confrontation of an American Jew with a whole country where the vast majority is Jewish—where Hebrew is the spoken language, where streets are named after famous events and persons in Jewish history, where one walks the very places where once walked our biblical forefathers, where once preached the Hebrew prophets, where the Jewish heroes of the past and present fought, and yet where all the complexity and technology of a modern state and a contemporary culture are to be found—has always had a very strong emotional impact on a young person. (Hayim Halevy Donin, *To Raise a Jewish Child*, p. 105)

THE COLLEGE EXPERIENCE

As graduation approaches, parents should advocate that their high-school children explore only those college options that include large, viable Jewish student populations, a Hillel Foundation, and nearby synagogue communities. Do not solely consider the math department or a college's prestige, but give equal weight to its Jewish life. Only colleges with substantial populations of Jewish students will provide an adequate selection of dating partners for your sons and daughters. The Hillel Foundation has evaluated Jewish student life on almost every campus in America. Consult the Hillel guide when beginning your college search.

There are questions your child—and you—must ponder when applying to colleges. Here is an adaptation of a questionnaire that appeared in the *Women's League Outlook* (Fall 1993):

How do I (teen and/or parent) feel about . . .

- going to a school with/without an active Jewish population?

- the presence/absence of a Hillel?

- the opportunity to keep kosher at school?

- a Jewish community for *Shabbat*, High Holy Days, Passover?

- mandatory/excused classes on Jewish holidays?

- availability/absence of Jewish studies courses?

- being able to study in Israel for credit?

- availability of Jewish fraternities or sororities?

- availability of kosher-for-Passover food?

- keeping up with friends from home, from your area?

- availability of Jewish students for dating partners?

- availability of KOACH [Conservative Jewish] activities on campus?(Richard Moline, "Choosing a College from a Jewish Perspective," pp. 21–22)

AFTER GRADUATION

Once a child has moved into the workplace, parents should actively provide information about Jewish singles programs. Lists of such programs are regularly featured in local Jewish newspapers and are also available from the regional United Synagogue office. Today more than ever, young adults are amenable to meeting one another in controlled settings. Remember that socialization and networking with other Jews are the keys for Jewish young adults to meet, date, and marry one another.

With these strategies in mind, nationally prominent Jewish educator Jonathan Woocher has observed:

> We know that Jewishness is a cumulative experience. The more one is involved in one aspect of being Jewish, the more likely one will be involved in others. The life narrative of many a Jewish success story describes a path from family to school to camp to youth group to Israel program to campus involvement to active Jewish adulthood. Some join the path along the way; some take detours or drop out for a time. The key is not to focus on any one experience, to seek the one decisive moment or program, but to lay the broad pavement along which the Jewish journey can proceed. (Jonathan Woocher, "Jewish Survival Tactics," p. 12)

3

It All Begins with a Date: Parent/Young Adult Dialogues about Interdating

One cause of interdating and ultimately intermarriage is parental silence in verbalizing the grounds for their concerns about the Jewishness of their family's future. Most of today's parents were raised in an atmosphere in which intermarriage was relatively uncommon. Teens grew up in Jewish neighborhoods. They encountered consistent messages of Jewish communal opposition to marrying outside the faith. Frowning upon interfaith socialization was echoed by Catholic and Protestant church circles as well.

Given this broad-based consensus of opposition to interdating and intermarriage, the previous generation of American Jewish moms and dads simply "bought into" that societal message. They did not have to articulate concrete reasons for their stance. Consequently, today's Jewish parents were never on the receiving end of substantive responses to the interdating and intermarriage questions that young adults of the 1990s now raise. Lacking memory of such replies, parents awkwardly avoid these topics.

In the absence of serious dialogue within family settings, sons and daughters grow into maturity assuming that *parental silence implies assent*. When Mom and Dad acquiesce to both interdating and to intermarriage, their offspring assume their parents accept the assimilationist assumptions of television, the film industry, and the campus.

Yet in reality, most Jewish parents greatly value Jewish continuity and hope for a Jewish future for their children and grandchildren. They oppose out-marriage but are ill at ease raising the issue. They are unclear how to fill these discussions with meaningful Jewish perspectives.

At the same time, many teens and college students are not ready to read about or discuss intermarriage. They quickly make clear that marriage, any marriage, "is the furthest thing from my mind." Their interests are focused on dating and they readily point out that dating has three components: simply having fun; developing social skills, security, poise, and maturity in relating to persons of the opposite sex; and romance.

So, they ask, "What is the problem with dating any person, regardless of his/her religion?" Dating, they say, is intended simply to have fun or to get to know others.

The following questions and answers are intended to assist dialogue about interdating in numerous settings, and they are designed for all concerned Jewish people, whether or not your family is religiously observant.

1. Mom/Dad, why are Jews so upset about interdating? Perhaps intermarriage is not acceptable, but dating simply means having a good time, without making a lifelong commitment. Why shouldn't I interdate until the right Jewish person comes along?

The danger with this line of reasoning is that dating cannot be so easily compartmentalized into separate stages: having fun, social maturation, romance, courtship, and then marriage can become a continuum. One stage *can* inadvertently *become* the next. Even if dating a specific individual does not lead to marrying that person, interdating can create a social pattern for the future. "The type of person who you say is okay to date today is more than likely to impact upon the type of person who you think is okay to date in the future when more serious relationships develop" (Joel Wasser, *We Are Family*, p. 45).

A date can certainly begin as an innocent outing. It can be part of a short-lived relationship, without any lasting implications for Jewish survival. However, the risk is what the *Parent Education Program* of United Synagogue of Conservative Judaism refers to as "the unpredictability of emotions."

> One cannot say it is "only a date" because, from that one date, one moves to solo dating with the individual. Nor can one assume that the non-Jewish partner will convert because "he/she loves me." He/she will probably say the same thing to his/her parents. Nor is it legitimate to say that "we will end it if it gets serious" because, when it gets serious, no one wants to end it. (*Parent Education for Parents of Adolescents*, vol. 3, p. 66)

As a parent you should make clear that having Gentile friends is great, but non-Jewish dating partners are risky. Once casual dating even unwittingly transforms into romantic love, it may be too late to reverse this perilous process. It is difficult to treat a relationship as a water faucet, merely turning the handle into the "off" position once "love" enters.

2. Come on. Isn't saying I won't interdate just another form of racism?

A rejection of interdating is not a question of being anti-democratic. "Democracy means treating everyone as equal before the law but it does NOT teach that one must, or even should . . . [forego] differences of belief and conviction"

(United Synagogue of Conservative Judaism, *Parent Education Program*, vol. 3, pp. 66–67). Nor is this *racial* bigotry! Judaism is not a race! There are Jews of all colors and ethnic backgrounds: from Ethiopia, India, Asia, Europe, Latin America, Middle Eastern countries, and so on.

Our opposition to interdating actually is a validation of the reality that Jews and non-Jews are *equally nice people*. We acknowledge that it *is possible* for a romantic attraction to a non-Jew to turn into a commitment to marriage once a process of dating has started.

One of my wife, Rita's, cousins related to me the experience on campus of being asked out on a date by a classmate named Jonathan Schwarz. Although Jonathan's name "sounded Jewish," the young lady asked Mr. Schwarz if indeed he was a Jew. The young man responded: "No. Why would that matter?" Rita's cousin appropriately answered:

> Jon, as a committed Jew, it is important to me that I marry another Jewish person. Since you are not Jewish, and you are such a terrific guy, someone with whom I could become romantically involved, it is critical that I do not accept your invitation for a date. We must not begin a process that might have to either end painfully for both of us or create an intermarriage.

Rabbi Charles Kroloff has noted: "The more you interdate, the more likely you are to marry a non-Jew. Dating is the process of sorting out your feelings about members of the opposite sex. But it also establishes patterns for socializing, delineates our group of friends, and presents the opportunity to be 'swept off our feet' " (Charles Kroloff, "Mixed Dating and Parents," p. 7). Rabbi Roland B. Gittelsohn describes the dynamic:

> You are not [necessarily] making your [specific] choice of a mate [by each interdate]. . . . But you are shaping your personality and

values; you are acquiring new knowledge and forming new attitudes; you are making important decisions . . . all of which will
eventually add up to your choice of a mate when the proper time
comes. . . . In this sense your attitudes and conduct [in dat-
ing] . . . have much to do with your choice of a spouse in the
future. (Roland B. Gittelsohn, *Love in Your Life*, p. 109)

In a conversation among teenagers with regard to interdating published in *The Jewish Family Book*, a young man named
Morty warned:

Don't say, "I'm just interdating, it's intermarriage I have to worry
about." At least be able to say to yourself, and to your parents, "I
am interdating, I am endangering the future of the Jewish people. . . . I may be a perfectly good, compassionate . . . human
being, but I am taking the chance that I will no longer be a serious
Jew." (Richard Israel, "Interdating," p. 352)

3. Aren't the criteria regarding dating different than those related to marriage?

It is understandable that you might assume that dating and
marriage are two totally separate realms. However, they are
linked by many subtle and unanticipated emotions and
complexities.

Romance assumes that love will bridge all difficulties, problems, and objective differences between two young people.
Such infatuation tends toward mutual idealization. That assumes that the partner is one's "ideal" mate, the only person
one could ever love.

Before young people even begin dating they have to be
reminded not to fall into the emotional traps of assuming
either that "love conquers all" or that "you can only love one
person." Neither myth is true. Romantic love, with its dating

and courtship, is superficial and unrealistic in comparison to the unavoidable complexities of family life. Because of this, dating may seem different, *but it sets patterns*. Once dating progresses into a serious relationship, each person reconnects to his or her family, ethnic, religious, and value system of birth. As sensitively portrayed in the film "Intermarriage: When Love Meets Tradition" (Union of American Hebrew Congregations, 1990), the loving couple gradually becomes aware of the extraordinary differences previously ignored.

In contrast to dating, marriage must confront complex realities. In *Intercultural Marriages: Promises and Pitfalls*, journalist Dugan Romano discusses the wide array of pitfalls potentially encountered by partners of different religious/cultural backgrounds once their relationship changes from dating/courtship (even living together) to marriage. If a person intermarries, every stage of marital life includes added potentials for strife. These new perils heap further complexity upon the already formidable mountain of challenges posed by contemporary family living (p. 28). Romano lists a wide variety of potential conflicts in an intermarriage, such as dealing with male/female roles, attitudes toward food and drink, religion, social class, child rearing, and ethnocentrism.

If dating leads to marriage, the life of any new household will be filled with unavoidable interpersonal and familial issues. Although a certain superficial excitement surrounds dating someone from a divergent background, if we are honest with ourselves, most of us acknowledge that further problems ultimately could ensue from an intermarriage. A non-Jewish husband or wife will not likely share such values as connections with your nuclear and extended Jewish family, ties to the Jewish community at large, feelings about Jews throughout the world, or an approach to God and Judaism.

Teens and college students often have some hesitancy about interdating. Adults can point out what the therapist Catherine Johnson advises: "The first piece of practical wisdom to emerge from the experiences of people who married 'wisely and well' is . . . when we meet someone we are dramatically drawn to, and some part of us is whispering 'No,' then no it should be" (Catherine Johnson, *Lucky in Love: The Secrets of Happy Couples and How Their Marriages Thrive,* p. 25).

4. Mom/Dad, what is the problem of interdating within our circle of non-Jewish friends? After all, we are just like one another in all other ways. Isn't it good to have non-Jewish friends?

BALANCING GENTILE FRIENDSHIPS WITH JEWISH DATING PATTERNS

It is well to acknowledge that it is certainly true that Jewish teens and college students are similar to their non-Jewish friends in many ways. They are all American citizens and share similar interests in sports, music, and pursuit of careers. Furthermore, it is praiseworthy for Jews of all ages to cultivate good friendships with persons of other backgrounds. However, maintaining a friendship is different from entering into the intimacy of dating—a one-to-one closeness that can lead ultimately to marriage.

I am aware of numerous congregations located in areas in which Jews are a tiny minority. The sons and daughters of committed Jewish families were raised with a peer group consisting primarily of non-Jews. Their closest friends were usually of different faith traditions, and their parents encouraged this camaraderie. However, there was one critical ground rule: friendship with non-Jewish persons is terrific, but dating is prohibited because it can lead to intermarriage. As a result, identifying Jews have grown up in such settings with life-long friendships among Catholics, Protestants, and the unchurched. These proud Jews forthrightly stated to their Christian buddies:

I very much value our friendships with each other, but in terms of the one-to-one intimacy of dating, my religion teaches that we should date only persons of the same faith. After all, dating can lead to romance, to engagement, and to marriage. And successful marriage should ideally involve two partners of the same religious background and commitment.

This clarity and integrity has been well respected by Gentile peers. Differentiating friendship from a date was a clear and respected boundary, admired by local residents. Unfortunately, this healthy ability to differentiate between friendship and dating is eroding. Youngsters now are asking: Why not interdate, if Jewish and Christian kids are all the same in every way?

DIFFERENCES DO EXIST

Teenagers in my community have described their feelings of alienation from Christian peers when mixed groups viewed movies with Jewish content such as *School Ties* and *Swing Kids*. *School Ties* offers a compelling case study of anti-Semitism in a high-school setting. *Swing Kids* portrays the powerful dilemmas faced by German youth during the rise of Nazism— whether to collaborate or to resist evil. In both instances, the Jewish viewers were profoundly moved by these films. In contrast, by and large, the Gentile friends reacted with indifference. As part of America's Christian majority, they could not relate to the main character in *School Ties*, a Jew who is subjected to social ostracism. Similarly, most of the non-Jews lacked interest in the Holocaust setting of *Swing Kids*. For them, the years of Hitler and of Nazi persecutions were not a concern. The Jewish students commented to me about their astonishment in realizing concrete ways in which they were truly different from their Christian friends.

In a similar fashion, I remember being a pre-med student at Cornell University and learning in early June 1967 that the

Arab states, led by Egypt, were threatening to "push Israel into the sea." For me, as a 19-year-old Jew, the thought of a second Holocaust, of the end of the State of Israel, sent shivers of fear and shock down my spine. In contrast, my Christian friends and classmates viewed this emerging crisis with the same apathy that all of us displayed to events in little-known corners of the globe. Israel, Jewish survival, the memory of the Holocaust, and the need to help fellow Jews in crisis turned out to be much more important to me than I had ever imagined. Yet, conversely, the indifference of my non-Jewish peers was more widespread than I could have guessed. Although we shared many career and entertainment interests, at the core of my very being, in terms of life and death moments, we were profoundly different.

THE DECEMBER DILEMMA

Jews also perceive religious symbols in different ways than their Christian contemporaries. This is most evident each December, as Christmas intrudes into our lives. Battles often occur at local school board meetings, town council sessions, and other civic gatherings. While Jews resent the flaunting of Christmas trees, wreathes, decorations, and songs in schools, town halls, the malls, and on television, Christians are offended by any attempts to separate Christmas from the public square. While we insist that our free and open society dictates the absence of one religion being *imposed* upon the daily life of all other Americans, Christians claim that their major holidays are not just religious but are part of "American culture." The inward reaction of Jews is: "They are not part of my culture." When one penetrates beneath agreement about music and sports and the quest for employment, teens and young adults generally find they differ passionately as Jews and Christians with regard to this "December dilemma."

Judaism and Christianity are not just about trees and *menorahs*. Jews differ from Christian friends and neighbors with regard to the specific religious tradition we rely upon during moments of crisis and stress. When young people die during high school or campus years, the specific Jewish, Catholic, or Protestant rituals of the deceased are invoked. When a parent is terminally ill, each of the religious traditions has its own distinct approach to fundamental decisions incumbent upon sons and daughters. What should be done regarding disconnecting life-support systems, organ donations, autopsies, cremation, and so on? Each religious group has its own unique beliefs with regard to abortion, birth control, genetic engineering, and a whole range of ethical issues. (See Appendix I for a review of the distinctions between Judaism and Christianity.)

Christians and Jews can and should become good friends. However, in terms of many paramount issues lurking beneath the surface of our daily lives, we are profoundly different from each other. Those differences should be respected.

5. I live in a Jewish community in which there are relatively few Jewish dating partners. Are you suggesting that I not date at all?

I am sensitive to the personal pain implied by your question. Certainly I want you to date and to develop the social skills that will lead toward a healthy Jewish marriage in your future. Nonetheless, strategies are available to achieve these goals as well as to maintain the religious integrity of dating only Jewish partners.

DEFERRING "FUN"

In some settings, meeting an eligible and suitable Jewish person *is difficult*. Nonetheless, Jewish teens and single adults should exercise restraint and avoid the peril of interdating. Short-term loneliness is better than a lifetime of difficulties.

AGGRESSIVELY TRAVEL TO NETWORK WITH OTHER JEWS

Jewish adolescents and young adults, particularly residents of small Jewish communities, should make added efforts to:

- attend regional youth (USY, KOACH, college, and young singles) gatherings;
- attend Jewish summer camps (as campers or staff);
- choose colleges and graduate schools with substantial numbers of Jewish students and vibrant Jewish student organizations;
- be receptive to blind dates;
- routinely visit relatives in neighborhoods with many Jews;
- become involved in Federation and UJA singles' divisions and other regional/national networks for bringing Jewish people together.

DO NOT PANIC

Even if a person opts for these appropriate choices, in the interim one may lack suitable Jewish dating partners. In spite of acknowledged difficulties, one must not panic in searching for fun and happiness. Panic can cause a Jew to become prey to rationalizations and to lose sight of the long-term implications of interdating and intermarriage in terms of future family, children, and descendants.

Momentary "fun" should not be confused with a lasting emotion such as happiness. Commentator Dennis Prager has written: "Fun is experienced only *during* an act. . . . [In contrast] happiness is experienced *after* an act" (Dennis Prager,

"Happiness Isn't Fun," p. 13). While fun can consist of indulging one's fleeting desires, enduring happiness must be connected to family, community, and religion, all of which are jeopardized by interdating and intermarriage.

6. Are all the television and film portrayals of compatible mixed dating and intermarriage off base?

Keep in mind the context of these television and film portrayals. The motivation of producers is to make a profit. To do so, they must gain ratings among the viewers. Consequently, the media projects what it regards as the most interesting, most marketable script, *not a carbon copy of reality*. Ninety-five percent of Americans, for example, indicate that they believe in God. We have been described as a "God-obsessed" society, and yet rarely do we ever see a media portrayal of spiritual concerns. Similarly, more than 60 percent of American citizens belong to a church or synagogue. Most Americans attend a prayer service several times per month. Yet how often is involvement in one's congregation or religious life made into the focus of films or TV dramas? Commercial sponsors are not interested in these topics. They are appealing to their biggest pool of consumers—teens and young, single adults—who are also experiencing the stage in life classically most distant from religious involvements. "Most recent Hollywood treatments of religion range from the disrespectful to vicious. . . . When not attacked, religion is usually treated as irrelevant" (see John Attarian's book review in *Crisis*).

Furthermore, some moguls of the Hollywood scene are notably in rebellion against traditional values. They consciously view the media as a means to challenge societal norms. Michael Medved concludes in his popular volume *Hollywood vs. America: Popular Culture and the War on Traditional Values*: "Rather than readjusting their view of reality . . . [to

accord with large percentages of] church attendance and affiliation . . . [their scripts] continue to write off all religious be-
lievers as . . . [country] bumpkins" (pp. 71–72).

In this context, it is no surprise that just as the media
trivializes the problems of dating, of sexual promiscuity in the
era of AIDS, of "cheating" on one's wife or husband, of drug
use, and of divorce, so too do they either ignore or sim-
plistically stereotype the deep, complex, and painful issues of
interdating and intermarriage. Ignoring Jewish uniqueness is
particularly desired by many of the secularized Jews who
inhabit Los Angeles's subculture of artistic expression.

> For the Jewish producers and writers of such shows, who
> [are] . . . seeking their own assimilation and acceptance into
> American culture, it [is] . . . useful to create characters who could
> demonstrate that there [is] . . . little difference between Jews and
> Christians, and that the distinct Jewish religion, culture, heritage
> and peoplehood [is] . . . in essence non-distinct. (Jonathan and
> Judith Pearl, "The Changing Channels of TV's Intermarriage De-
> pictions," *Jewish Televimage Report*, p. 1)

Thus, popular TV shows have prominent characters who
interdate or are intermarried and who never seem to experience difficulties in their mixed-religion settings. Similar bliss-
ful portrayals of mixed dating and marriage are included in
films.

Nevertheless, signs are appearing of a break in this mono-
lithic depiction of the alleged perfect joys of intermarriage, as
more Jewishly identifying writers and producers develop
scripts. The popular television series *Thirtysomething* included
several episodes in which the Jewish husband, the lead character, agonized over whether to celebrate Hanukkah, Christmas,
or both; whether to provide a *bris* ceremony for his son; and
whether to say *Kaddish* in a local synagogue for his father.
Another television hit, *Sisters*, sensitively portrayed the conversion to Judaism by a primary character, a non-Jewish wife

on the verge of motherhood, influenced by the positive religious commitments of her mother-in-law. The series *Commish* offered the thoughtful decision by an intermarried couple to raise their child as a Jew rather than "in both religions." Accordingly, the family chose to celebrate Hanukkah and to omit Christmas from their home.

In the movies, Sidney Lumet's *Stranger Among Us* introduced a previously unimaginable, praiseworthy Hollywood assessment of the interior lives of hasidic Jews. Gentile lead Melanie Griffith admiringly experienced the positive family life of traditional Jews, in contrast to the tragic break-up of her own secularized family. *Crossing Delancey* found Amy Irving gradually realizing that true marital happiness can be found best by marrying someone of her own religious background and rejecting the seductive appeal of a non-Jewish suitor.

The media's need for profit and the assimilationist desires of some Jewish writers and producers have to be kept in mind when their biased portrayals of interdating and intermarriage are viewed. Film experts Jonathan and Judith Pearl comment: "Where are TV's Jewish-Jewish relationships [i.e., 75 percent of households in which Jews live]? Their underrepresentation on TV not only omits an important reality, but sends the message to *young Jewish viewers* that dating one's coreligionist is not 'cool' " (Jonathan and Judith Pearl, "The Changing Channels of TV's Intermarriage Depictions," p. 1).

7. I have another issue to raise. Jewish prospective dating partners don't seem to have the qualities I seek.

If a Jewish person believes that only Gentiles are attractive dating partners, if one claims that all Jews are incapable of being suitable people to date and ultimately to marry, then perhaps a subconscious motivation is at work. Jews sometimes project the ills of their own family onto all other Jewish people, thereby creating an aversion to setting up yet one more Jewish home. Therapist Esther Perel has observed:

> Sometimes . . . negative feelings toward Jewishness have to do [with one's] . . . family dynamic. When the emotional processes in the family are very intense, people find it difficult to separate their feelings about their Jewishness from their feelings about family. . . . The parents are often the children's sole or primary representatives of what Judaism is, so if they want to leave the parents they often feel that they have to leave Judaism as well. (Esther Perel, "A More Perfect Union: Intermarriage and the Jewish World," *Tikkun*, pp. 61–62)

Professor Monica McGoldrick, who is an expert in ethnotherapy, which helps people resolve these internal psychological conflicts, has written: "[Those who intermarry may be] seeking a rebalance of the characteristics of their own ethnic background. . . . During courtship [therefore] a person may be attracted precisely to the fiance's differentness, but when entrenched in a marital relationship the same qualities often become the rub" (cited in Paul and Rachel Cowan, *Mixed Blessings*, p. 130).

Because the rejection of Jews as dating partners can be fraught with complicated psychodynamics, this may be an area with which it is very difficult for a parent or relative to deal. This is an area in which other adults can often play an important role.

It is always in order to raise one's consciousness about the prejudices underlying damaging JAPs (Jewish American Princesses and Princes) stereotyping. One common trap into which single Jews fall is the temptation to feel part of American society's negative assessment of Jews, female and male, as JAPs. The JAP is accused of being uniquely materialistic, spoiled, and sexually prudish. Esther Perel states: "[Intermarrying] Jewish men and women tend to project negative stereotypes about Jews onto each other and make them gender bound. In this way they dissociate themselves from the stereotype. . . . It's as if they are thinking, 'If I'm not with you, I'm not like you' " (Esther Perel, "A More Perfect Union: Intermarriage and the Jewish World," p. 61).

As a trigger for group discussion, a B'nai B'rith Women's audiocassette tape relates the following brutally harsh comedian's parody of the so-called JAP:

> A Jewish American Princess is a special kind of royalty, reigning supremely but justly over her vast domain. She is the sovereign of Saks, the monarch of Magnin, the princess of Pappagallo, the countess of Cartier, the guru of Gucci, the sultan of Sasson, the baalabosta of Bergdorf, the lord of Taylor.
>
> The Jewish American Princess can do everything. She can mop, clean, dust, vacuum, make a bed, scrub a floor and scour an oven. But thank God, she'll never have to! The Jewish American Princess can ride a horse, ski, play tennis, jog three miles in a rubber suit and never sweat. But thank God, she'll never have to! The Jewish American Princess has a magnificent bedroom, with flecked paper, a brass headboard, a king-sized bed and seven sex manuals. But thank God, she'll never have to! (B'nai B'rith Women, "The Image of the Jewish Woman: Myth and Reality," audiocassette and discussion guide)

Equally commonplace and harmful are popular books of insults against Jewish women, such as *The Official J.A.P. Handbook*. This sleazy volume includes the following accusations:

> The born JAP knows that she is a treasure, does not waste her time on unworthy [in terms of status] men. . . . [By age] seventeen, she has had the requisite plastic surgery (nose job, breast reduction, or breast augmentation), owns a fur coat, diamond earrings, has been to Europe . . . truly believes that she is one of the loveliest and brightest creatures ever to have graced God's earth.

At the core of her [belief system] . . . are two guiding principles: 1) I am terrific; 2) Daddy will pay. (Anna Sequoia, *The Official J.A.P. Handbook*, pp. 11–12)

Given an American culture where Jewish women are vilified as the bearers of these negative qualities, it is not surprising that, in Paul and Rachel Cowan's workshops with Jewish men married to Gentile women, images of JAPs surfaced again and again. To justify their rejection of a prospective Jewish mate, these intermarried men described Jewish females as "possessive, materialistic, domineering, intrusive, overbearing, talkative, concerned with looks, status and success-oriented" (Paul and Rachel Cowan, *Mixed Blessings*, p. 171). Numerous intermarried Jewish men have shared similarly defensive rationalizations with me, claiming that Jewish girls are "too demanding" and are "always nagging you to do better." They make you "feel like you never quite measure up."

In contrast, in keeping with the ethos of American society, these same Jewish guys have romanticized images of non-Jewish women. Mocking this bitter reality, Woody Allen has joked:

WASP [women] are the girls whose older brothers are the engaging, good-natured, confident, clean, swift and powerful halfbacks for the college football teams called Northwestern, Texas Christian and UCLA. Their fathers are men with white hair and deep voices who never use double negatives; and their mothers the ladies with the kindly smiles and wonderful manners who say things like, "I do believe, Mary, that we sold thirty-five cakes at the bake sale." (Moshe Waldoks, *The Big American Book of Jewish Humor*, p. 101)

In the same vein, at the Cowans's sessions, intermarried Jewish men liked Gentile women because they were "blond, adventurous, undemanding, quieter and more supportive"

(Paul and Rachel Cowan, *Mixed Blessings*, p. 172). My contacts with intermarried couples have included some Jewish husbands who have described their wives as "pretty and soft," with relatives tracing their roots back to colonial times.

Exhibiting similar biases against Jewish males and toward Gentile men, intermarried Jewish women subscribed to the American anti-Jewish stereotype of the "Jewish American Prince." According to this canard: From the time he is a very young man, the prince knows he is "God's gift to American womanhood." He prefers a non-Jewish woman who will devote herself totally to his happiness, in contrast to the mutuality and career aspirations of Jewish women.

In the discussions facilitated by Paul and Rachel Cowan, intermarried Jewish women rejected Jewish men as "Mama's boys, balding and potbellied, lawyers and doctors from Long Island . . . brainy, scrawny and thin, unathletic . . . neurotic, insecure" (Paul and Rachel Cowan, *Mixed Blessings*, p. 171). Jewish men, these women said, "all want to be mothered. I don't know what their problem is, but with a Christian man you know who wears the pants in the family" (Paul and Rachel Cowan, *Mixed Blessings*, p. 44). A mixed-married Jewish woman once told me: "Jewish men are too concerned about pleasing their parents. They cannot let go of the apron strings."

As expected in the context of such damaging stereotypes, intermarried Jewish women have a romanticized view of Gentile men and speak of them as "athletic, fun, caring, good looking, loving but not overbearing" (Paul and Rachel Cowan, *Mixed Blessings*, p. 172). One such Jewish woman related that she had chosen "an Adonis," a "football player" who would be able to "take care of her"—a "Woody Allen" (i.e., a Jewish man) just would not do.

By projecting the worst anti-Jewish images of the American ethos upon prospective Jewish mates and at the same time romanticizing the positive attributes of Gentile partners, many Jewish men and women make dating Jews an impossibility.

Materialism, insensitivity, and selfishness can occur in some Jewish women. Self-centeredness and weakness of character are possible among Jewish men. However, neither Jewish males nor females have a monopoly on these liabilities. Plenty of Christians display similar foibles.

Moreover, the positive qualities of a caring, nurturing, yet strong spouse most certainly can be found within the Jewish community, just as easily as within the Gentile world. And Jewish partners also have the *benefits* of a *shared* background, a *shared* heritage, a *shared* religious tradition. If one does not agree with the obvious social reality that suitable Jewish partners *do exist*, then perhaps he/she is subconsciously projecting negative qualities upon other Jewish people.

8. Why do you (parents/grandparents) interfere in this aspect of my decision-making? This is my life, isn't it? Why can't you be like other parents and leave me alone? Why do you care so much about intermarriage when you are not religious anyway?

Parental responsibility is part of the Jewish tradition. The Jewish tradition does not support the notion that parents should abstain from expressing opinions to their teenage or adult offspring. Although children do not like to hear that their parents disagree with them, the commandment in the Torah is "Thou shalt *teach* them [the imperatives of Judaism] to your children." This means that whenever a son or daughter is engaged in an activity of which Judaism disapproves, a mother and/or father, albeit *respectfully*, must express their disapproval.

This is all the more so in the case of interdating and intermarriage. After all, marrying outside the Jewish community impacts not only upon the son or daughter but upon the parents. They too will be faced with the entry of a non-Jew into their extended family. Parents realistically are concerned with the probability that their dreams and expectations of future Jewish grandchildren who will continue the *chain of tradition* will never come to pass.

Concerned mothers and fathers are well aware of the implications of remaining silent about interdating and intermarriage. Silence might well be interpreted as assent or agreement. Let your son and daughter know that you consider it your obligation to make your position clear. Besides, taking a position is effective, as Rabbi Richard Israel wrote: "The highest percentage of intermarriage belongs to those whose parents approve of interdating. . . . If you don't approve of interdating [and articulate this disapproval], your children may intermarry anyway . . . [however] the statistics [the probabilities] are lower" (Richard Israel, "Interdating," p. 350).

Disapproval is unpleasant, so make it clear that you love your child. It would be much easier for you simply to agree at all times with their decisions, avoiding any prospect of confrontation. For Judaism, the parental role is not to be a friend to your children, but to be a good parent, which frequently involves being the bearer of unpopular counterviews.

As for the second question, he/she is right! Far too many parents *are* silent about interdating/intermarriage. However, this is not because they necessarily agree with mixed marriage and its implications, but because they are uncomfortable articulating what they know in their hearts is true. In a recently published guide to assist parents in asserting their role, Rabbis Mark Winer and Aryeh Meir have stated:

> We believe that there are parents who would express opposition to intermarriage but lack the language to communicate their feelings. What is needed is a language of endogamy—i.e., a means of communicating what they think and feel about what they value and find meaningful and unique in their Jewishness. They know they want their grandchildren to be Jewish. They know they want their children and their families to identify with the Jewish people

and its heritage. They want to be sure that the long chain of Jewishness, passed down through so many generations, will not be lost forever. They want this Jewishness preserved, even though they may not [be able to express] why. (Mark Winer and Aryeh Meir, original draft of *Questions Jewish Parents Ask About Intermarriage: A Guide for Jewish Families*, p. 2)

Jewish parents are committed to Jewish survival, whether or not they are observant. The third inquiry—about parents who are not personally religious caring so much about intermarriage—shows a misunderstanding about the nature of Judaism. Christianity was established according to the Greco-Roman concept of "religia." "Religia" implies a very narrow aspect of an individual's life. It means the spiritual dimension of one human being's existence—prayer, ceremonial rituals, sermons. It is confined to religious buildings such as churches and to rare religious moments such as prayer. In contrast, predating Christianity by 1,500 years, Judaism has never been confined to "religia" alone. Instead, Judaism implies a religious approach to *all* facets of life and takes place in a communal context of Jewish peoplehood and family.

A nonpracticing Christian is accurately regarded as "unchurched," as being part of no religious faith whatsoever. In contrast, the definition of Judaism solely as a faith community was never applicable. Jews are well aware that in addition to ritual practices and prayers, we are bound together as a tradition, a heritage, a culture, a peoplehood. Rabbi Mordecai Kaplan taught that we are a "religious civilization." We possess "a feeling of belonging to a historic and indivisible people, rooted in a common land, a continuing history, a living language [Hebrew] and literature, and common mores, laws and arts, with religion as the integrating and soul-giving factor" (Mordecai Kaplan, *The Future of the American Jew*, pp. 35–36).

As a religious civilization, Judaism believes that all past, present, and future Jews, both born Jews and Jews by Choice (converts), were present spiritually at Mount Sinai to receive the Torah. We are not simply individuals in communion at times with God but are part of a collectivity, *Am Yisrael*, the Jewish peoplehood. We have always felt and will continue to value linkages with fellow Jews throughout the world and throughout history. Consequently, the historic institution of the synagogue was never reduced solely to being a church-like locale for "religia."

On the contrary, authentic Jewish congregations always have retained their function as a *bet knesset*, a Jewish center for all aspects of the lifetime of each Jew and for every genre of Jewish group. In our day, this "house of assembly" function can be seen in the existence of Sisterhoods, Men's Clubs, youth groups, senior citizen programs, adult education, support groups (for the bereaved, for divorcees, for single parents, and for the unemployed), parenting centers, *chavurot* (family networking), and so on. To be a good member of the congregation means to be involved in the religious and/or *bet knesset* dimensions of the synagogue. Furthermore, the local synagogue exists within a larger Jewish community as well, with Federation and UJA offering aid to distressed Jews in Israel and throughout the world. Jews participate in a religious civilization, a religion tied to a sense of peoplehood.

There are diverse modes of Jewish commitment. Being part of "a religious civilization in action," individual Jews—whether observant or not—have never relinquished pride in or loyalty to our unique and indispensable Jewish heritage. All types of Jews have seen the value of preserving Judaism's unprecedented 3,500-year chain of tradition and the diverse contributions of Jews to the world's religious, legal, scholarly, and moral life.

The scholar of Judaica Gershom Sholem once observed that, unlike our Christian neighbors, who are either "religious" or "unchurched," our Jewish world is composed of "Hand Jews," "Head Jews," and "Heart Jews." "Heart Jews" feel an affinity for Jewish rituals, spirituality, symbols, and belief systems as "religious" Jews. "Head Jews" are inspired by Jewish books, ideas, scholarship, openness to inquiry, and richness of thinking. "Hand Jews" respond to hands-on acts of philanthropy, of aiding the hungry, the homeless, the ill and the emotionally isolated, and the politically vulnerable brethren such as Israelis, Russian Jews, Ethiopian Jews, and so on. Thus "Heart Jews," "Hand Jews," and "Head Jews" all appreciate the value of Jewish community and continuity.

Whether or not you practice rituals or frequently attend synagogue services, you fit comfortably into other meaningful slots of Jewish identity and involvement. You might care deeply about transmitting Jewish heritage, values, communal ties, and a religious approach to birth, life, death, and ethical dilemmas to your children and your future offspring. Your children should not be surprised by, nor offended at, your interest and concern. It is both genuine and authentic.

9. Mom/Dad, aren't you being hypocrites about interdating and intermarriage? After all, you attended my cousin's intermarriage wedding. You accept Aunt Jane and Uncle Ralph's marriage, even though they had interdated and then Jane converted to Judaism. You even accept Aunt Sarah and Uncle John's family. Though John never relinquished his Christianity, their kids are being raised as Jews.

No! You are not hypocrites. You would be hypocrites if you told your children that we were not attending your cousin's wedding, and behind their backs actually did so. Or you would be hypocrites if you swore that because Uncle John has not converted to Judaism, you will not visit Sarah and John's home, and then secretly ignore your vow. Rather than being hypocrites, you are being very honest about what you accept and what you do not.

My advice to parents is to more clearly verbalize one's parental point of view. Parents should share with their sons and daughters exactly how they have reconciled acceptance of intermarrieds within the family while still opposing interdating and intermarriage for their offspring.

There is a difference between what is expected of Jews "in advance of their actions" and coping with unapproved behavior "after the fact." It is right to express disapproval when Jane and Ralph, Sarah and John were interdating. We have warned that a date can and does gradually shift into romance, love, and then marriage.

Yet after the fact, we appreciate that Jane has converted to Judaism. But we also know that conversion by a non-Jewish spouse occurs in less than 5 percent of interfaith marriages. We also know that a convert cannot simply be "left dripping at the *mikveh*." Ongoing challenges will still confront conversionary households—they will have to resolve relationships with Gentile relatives; they will have to create memories for the Jew by Choice. Although achievable, the route to creating an undiluted Jewish identity is difficult for such a Jewish family.

Similarly, we are pleased that Sarah and John have decided to raise their children as Jews, but we also realize that more than 70 percent of boys and girls in mixed homes are not raised as Jews. Furthermore, we understand that in Sarah and John's mixed-married household, the decision to raise a child as a Jew is merely the first in a lifetime of hurdles that will arise. They will face an uphill battle in nurturing a youngster with clear messages about Jewish identity.

In other words, after the fact, we—as family members—are respectful of efforts by relatives to cope with difficult realities created by interdating and intermarriage. However, parental respect for these uphill efforts to cope should not be confused with parental preference for, or approval of, dating or marrying non-Jews.

Whether or not you have relatives who are involved in interdating or intermarriage, the wisdom garnered by decades of encounters with the difficulties of such relationships validates the position of the Jewish tradition: Jews should date and marry Jews! That wisdom appears in a letter Rabbi Perry Rank wrote to college students from his community of Springfield, New Jersey, in 1990 in which he addressed his opposition to interdating and the importance of finding a Jewish mate.

My concern with Jewish endogamy does not mean that I want Jews to be cliquish. I would never want you to give up your non-Jewish friends or treat them with less deference. . . . I, like you, do not think Jews are inherently better or smarter than anyone else. . . .

Nevertheless, as special as you are . . . as a promising professional, [businessperson, etc.] . . . you are also special by virtue of your Jewishness. This religion confers upon us all sorts of time-honored traditions and obligations designed to bring a little *tikkun* (social reformation) and *k'dushah* (sanctity) into the world.

That mission is as honorable as it is overwhelming. You will need help. And the help you receive comes best from a spouse who both understands the mission and feels equally bound to it as you.

4

Planting Seeds for Jewish Continuity:
A Guide for Children Ages 3–6

In generations past, a firm Jewish identity could be assumed. As Tevye said in "Fiddler on the Roof," in a fashion that applied as well to the previous generations of Jews of Brooklyn, Queens, Northeast Philadelphia, Shaker Heights (a suburb of Cleveland), and Oak Park (a suburb of Detroit): "We knew who we were. We knew our place in society."

Times have changed. We live in a world of unlimited choices and social turmoil. Jewish parents are raising children in an environment that poses serious challenges to the Jewish future of their families. Jewish children are minorities in their neighborhoods and public schools. Jewish ethnic distinctiveness is eroding. Jews intermarry at ever-increasing rates.

Much more so than in previous generations, young parents concerned with the long-term Jewish future of their children and grandchildren must create a personal strategy that maximizes the prospect of Jewish continuity. Just as youngsters ages 3 to 6 begin to be presented with all other valued aspects of living, so too must parents systematically promote Jewish identity.

Your children will choose their values when they become mature, with or without your permission. What choices they make and, more importantly, how they make those choices, will depend more than anything upon the direction they receive from you in their younger years. (Jack Moline, "Ten Things We Do Not Say Often Enough to Our Children," audiotape)

1. Rabbi, how can we answer the question "Why be Jewish?" both for kids and for ourselves?

In terms of self-fulfillment, the arena of greatest concern in American culture, Judaism offers "gains" for all types of Jewish needs.

Spiritually, for children ages 3 to 6, Judaism's rich legacy includes ritual circumcision (*bris*), baby naming, nursery school, commencing Jewish education, *Shabbat*, Simchat Torah, Hanukkah, Purim, and a host of other experiences in our quest for God's presence.

Intellectually, Jewish sacred texts are distilled as bedtime stories, age-appropriate books, magazines, videotapes, computer programs, and music.

Ethically, Jewish social action offers youngsters the chance to join their parents in visiting the sick, welcoming the newcomer (immigrant, guest) to their homes, placing coins in the *tzedakah* box to aid the hungry and the homeless, and witnessing family members' voluntarism in Jewish and civic institutions.

Judaism also offers personal meaning to us by connecting each Jew with profound commitments to the age-old Jewish tradition, to Jews throughout the world, and to God. (See chapter 5 for a full discussion of "Why Be Jewish?")

2. Are parents really important role models for the transmission of Judaism to their offspring?

Don't underestimate the powerful influence your words and actions have on your children.

Much of our education is unintended. Much of it is also unanticipated. . . . Education happens in the margins of life, in the casual remark and in the small incident. We are teaching [our children] at every moment, whether we want to or not. The only question is what we will teach. What children remember is often quite different from what we planned. That is why teaching religion must be done not in careful, specified settings [by formal teachers alone], but all the time [i.e., by parents]. Faith must be lived. (David J. Wolpe, *Explaining God to Children: A Jewish Perspective*, p. 25)

Recently a Jewishly concerned mother of small children recounted her amazement at overhearing her 5-year-old daughter playing house with a neighbor. As the two youngsters discussed their imaginary households, my friend's daughter proudly described the Friday night *Shabbat* dinner and ritualized Saturday morning family outing to the local synagogue, as well as a range of holiday moments including building a *sukkah*, lighting Hanukkah candles, and partaking in Passover *seders*. Although this child frequently objects to her parents' insistence upon Jewish ritual practices and synagogue attendance, clearly she was internalizing their values.

Be a role model for your children in word and deed. Parents can use some of the ideas prepared by the Rabbinic Advisory Council of UJA/Federation of New York on "10 Ways to Enhance Your Jewish Identity":

1. Invest yourself. Make the time and commitment to enhance yourself Jewishly.

2. Share your Jewish journey with friends in a community context.

3. Seek opportunities for serious study to increase your knowledge and to gain intellectual awareness and historical perspective.

4. Seek a religious/spiritual component to your life.

5. Pray every day with both a meditative and intellectual contemplation.

6. Say the blessings for food, and turn your table into an altar.

7. Make the Sabbath and holidays holy. Enhance them with rituals at home and at the synagogue.

8. Involve your family.

9. Be aware of and involved in Jewish causes. Don't separate yourself from the community.

10. Make a pilgrimage to Israel.

When children watch parents seriously involved in aspects of Jewish life, they realize that Judaism is important to all stages of life. Author Dennis Prager stated in a speech on "Raising a Jewish Child in a Christian Society":

> If adults take Judaism seriously, children take Judaism seriously. . . . If you stop Jewish education at age 13, a child will always identify Judaism with being a child. They will feel that sophisticated people study anthropology, political science, psychology . . . [in contrast] children watch cartoons and study Judaism. . . . If a parent takes Judaism seriously, it is a powerful message to a child. (Dennis Prager, "Raising a Jewish Child in a Christian Society," audiotape)

3. Does remaining Jewish require that I segregate my children from society, as do some Jewish groups?

No! The choices are not either to succumb to self-segregation or to assimilate. It is unrealistic to cloister ourselves in segregated neighborhoods. However, it is also undesirable to simply surrender our Jewish religious heritage to a "melting pot" of undifferentiated Americans citizens. This is *not* the greatness of our country's heritage. American life encourages each group to *acculturate*—to adopt American cultural norms (the English language, American civic culture) while preserving the group's faith, traditions, and values.

To teach our children to acculturate means to instruct them to be both American and Jewish with equal pride and seriousness, to be civicly identified with the United States and fellow Americans and to be tied religiously with Judaism and Jewish coreligionists. This creative living in *two civilizations* should be articulated and continually modeled for our children.

For example, we urge our children to grow up and be successful in their chosen careers: "Be a good doctor, lawyer, and so on." Along with this aspiration, we also must say with equal conviction, "Be a good Jew. Be a *mensch.*" Our children must see that we follow the civil and Jewish calendars of holidays and celebrations with equal fervor. Boys and girls ought to observe that Jewish ritual items, books, art, and music are given equal prominence with American cultural trends.

Similarly, just as we insist that they study hard and do well in their secular subjects (math, science, social studies, English), so too must we insist that they apply themselves with equal effort to Jewish subjects in synagogue Hebrew schools or Jewish day schools. Just as we would never ask a child if he or she wants to go to secular school, *do not ask if your child wants to go to "Jewish" school.* Just as we would never permit our youngster to "cut" secular school for a birthday party or gymnastics practice, so too must we forbid "cutting" religious school for similar extracurricular activities.

Later, children must learn to have the *courage to speak up as proud Jews* and to tell their Little League or cheerleading coach of a time conflict between their scheduled practice or game and a Jewish religious school or holiday commitment. Do not allow your child to meekly ignore the Jewish agenda or to give outside activities priority above Judaism.

We need to convey that both American and Jewish involvements are important so that acculturation—a midpoint between isolation and assimilation—and a synthesis of American and Jewish involvement will be possible for our children.

4. Rabbi, give me an example of this synthesis when the annual December dilemma, Hanukkah vs. Christmas, invades our family's life!

Although it may be difficult to explain to very young children, tell them that America encourages people both to be involved with their *own* religious traditions and to be respectful of the holidays of other people as well. A valuable resource in this parenting process is "The December Dilemma" section in Ron Wolfson's book *The Art of Jewish Living: Hanukkah*.

> When we live side-by-side with other religious people, we must respect and appreciate their customs, art and traditions. . . . What does appreciation mean? It means that there is nothing wrong with enjoying the beauty of someone else's celebration. . . . If we are strong in our Jewish commitments, there is little danger that approaching the warmth and beauty of another's holiday will threaten our fundamental identity. But appreciation does not mean appropriation. Because appropriation leads to confusion, loss of identity and, ultimately, assimilation. (Ron Wolfson, *The Art of Jewish Living: Hanukkah*, p. 173)

Although Christmas is powerfully present in malls, television ads, and programming, it is a valuable lesson for Jewish children to learn the message of Hanukkah—that Maccabees were unwilling to relinquish their unique religious way of life even though the vast majority of other people celebrated in a Greek cultural fashion.

> There are parents who believe that the December lesson that Jews are different than almost everybody else is an inescapable part of being Jewish, unless you live in Israel. There is a great value in being unique, different, valuable in your own right. . . . They want their children to identify with the Maccabees' struggle for religious liberty and for the right *not* to assimilate into the majority culture. Is this not the very same struggle that we Jews living in a predominantly Christian society must also wage? (Ron Wolfson, *The Art of Jewish Living: Hanukkah*, p. 173)

This is also a perfect occasion to teach the perils of peer pressure and of standing up for one's personal principles, whether or not this behavior will be popular. Jewish educator Joel Grishaver tells a related story regarding a child who was upset about being different in school and trying to explain Hanukkah to peers.

> His father hugs him and says: "Jews are different from other people. We don't do everything that everybody else does. We have our own important things. Our holiday is Chanukah and Chanukah is a holiday about being different. When Antiochus wanted the Jews to do everything that everyone else did and not be different, the Maccabees had to fight to get their freedom. Chanukah teaches us to remember that Jews are different. . . .
>
> "I want you to be special and different from everyone else. I love you. When you get older and everyone else does things like smoke or drink or take drugs, I want you to know that you can be different. When everyone else you know forgets to be kind to other people, I want you to be kind. When everyone else is afraid to stand up for what is right, I want you to be the one who leads people to do the right thing. Never forget, you are different and special." (Joel Grishaver, "December Dilemma," p. 3)

I remember when my son reached age 3 and asked of me the inevitable question: "Dad, how come we don't celebrate Christmas?" "David," I answered him, "Christmas is a great holiday for Christian people. However, if we celebrated Christmas, we would be Christian people, and so we would not have our great holidays—Rosh Hashanah, Sukkot, Simchat Torah, Hanukkah, Tu b'Shvat, Purim, Passover, Israeli Independence Day." Or, as one of my congregants told her child: "Sammy, it is like a birthday party. Sometimes, you go to someone else's party and say, 'This is great.' But it is not *your* party. But don't worry, your party will come. Christmas is not our holiday, but our holidays are great and we have them all year long!" Ron Wolfson writes:

> The child who has experienced the building of a *sukkah* will not feel deprived of trimming a tree. The child who had participated in a meaningful Passover Seder will not feel deprived of Christmas dinner. The child who has paraded with the Torah on Simchat Torah, planted trees at Tu b'Shvat, brought first fruits at Shavuot, given *mishloah manot* at Purim, and welcomed the Shabbat weekly with candles and wine and challah, by the time s/he is 3 years old will understand that to be Jewish is to be enriched by a calendar brimming with joyous celebration. (Ron Wolfson, *The Art of Jewish Living: Hanukkah*, p. 173)

5. What shall we say when youngsters ask about intermarriage, about intermarried relatives, about people they know who are interdating, about television shows in which people are married to persons of different religious backgrounds?

Once again a synthesis is necessary. If we are truly concerned about transmitting Jewish continuity to future generations, then we must be honest and offer clarity of views, from the earliest of ages. As Rabbi Jack Moline has said:

How is it that we open a savings account for our children when they are born to save for college, but we consider it too soon to discuss married life until a kid is already suspicious about what we say? How is it that . . . when they are playing bride and groom we hesitate to ask, "Where is the *chuppah*? Where is the *ketubah*? (Jack Moline, "Ten Things We Do Not Say Often Enough to our Children," audiotape)

Here, as with the differences between Judaism and Christianity, background information is important. As children get older, unpack these concepts into age-appropriate concepts and phrasing.

First, we must create a positive attitude in our home toward persons who have sincerely converted to Judaism. In actions as well as in adult conversations, children should see and hear their parents treating "converts" as full-fledged Jews.

We must embody the important message that a marriage between a born Jew and a Jew by Choice is not an intermarriage. However, later on, as the child approaches a higher stage of comprehension, we ought to point out clearly to our sons and daughters that conversion by a non-Jewish spouse, while praiseworthy, is highly unusual.

Second, in our behavior and our adult discussions, we can applaud non-Jewish spouses who are supportive of raising their children as synagogue members, as students in Hebrew schools, and as committed Jews. However, as they mature, we must show our offspring that this too is quite exceptional.

Third, given such high risks against Jewish continuity posed by intermarriage, we must specify that the Torah and Jewish tradition want Jewish people to marry other Jewish people because that is by far that best guarantee of creating Jewish homes and rearing future Jewish children.

As for intermarried cousins or other relatives, we must articulate to our offspring as they mature: "There is a difference between our preference that cousin Sarah would have married a Jewish man, and the reality after the fact that she did not. Although before Sarah was married we hoped that she would have a Jewish marriage, we still love her and love her family. Nevertheless, we continue to believe that Judaism teaches us to marry people with whom we can best share in creating a new Jewish home."

In terms of interdating or having friendships with non-Jews, we should instruct even young children: "Since it is important for Jewish people to marry other Jewish people and create Jewish homes, we do not approve of interdating. Having friendships with non-Jewish boys and girls is terrific, but dating can lead to romance, to love, and to marriage." Again citing the warnings of Jack Moline:

> A clear and articulate message of the ground rules regarding interdating is essential long before your child's first kiss. I don't think it is ever too early to distinguish between friendship and love. . . . *If you are hugging and kissing someone, it defines that relationship as one with long-term potential.* (Jack Moline, "Ten Things We Do Not Say Often Enough to Our Children," audiotape)

As for television, it intrudes into our family lives. Children should be taught early in life not to regard television as a source of right and wrong. In language suitable to their years, we should instruct our sons and daughters that television is intended to excite the viewer by offering dramatic events. However, that excitement—with excessive violence, with husbands and wives being disloyal to one another, with people doing all kinds of dishonest things—should never become our source of values.

Issues of interdating and intermarriage should be discussed and clarified early in childhood, at the point that Jewish boys and girls individually become aware of these phenomena. Do not hesitate to discuss dating and marital religious issues, or your children will interpret your silence as assent.

6. What other matters must we resolve in our own minds as parents before we can teach our children to have pride as Jews?

As Jews seeking a balance between assimilation and isolation for our families, we must be prepared to confront the secular canards that claim that loyalty to Judaism is inconsistent with modern living:

- Judaism is "outdated, and does not keep up with the times."

- Judaism "emphasizes ritual to the exclusion of ethics."

- Judaism's "view of prayer is limited to fixed texts by rote rather than spontaneous outpourings of the heart."

- Judaism "demands too much time from the already over-worked American life-style."

We may not always feel emotionally ready to deal with these issues, but we should be prepared to counter these accusations for our own benefit and the benefit of our children.

First, Judaism teaches us to adhere to both tradition and change. Just as the growth of a plant must be in harmony with the existing shrub to thrive, so too religious life will grow if it experiences healthy change in harmony with tradition.

Second, the Jewish religion is premised upon both ritual and ethics. For example, the dietary laws (*kashrut*) are sometimes denigrated as being solely ritual, i.e., irrelevant to the moral sensitivities of modern persons. However, the intent of *kashrut* is both ritual and moral. Keeping kosher is an ethical imperative—not to hunt, not to cause excessive suffering to animal life, and to recognize that eating meat is a moral compromise that should be done with restraint and sanctity. Moreover, the laws of *kashrut* teach us and our children the ethical benefits of learning to restrain our appetites. We cannot take and eat everything we desire; there are limits. In an age of affluence, leading to substance abuse, overeating, and addictions, this is all the more a critical lesson.

Third, Jewish ritual, notably Jewish prayer, includes both "rote" (fixed prayers) and "spontaneity." Judaism recognizes that there is an important contribution to one's spiritual life to be played by spontaneous, personal communion with God. Yet Judaism also stresses the blessing of fixed prayer, which serves us so well in times of need. A mourner, for example, by reciting the fixed *Kaddish*, is able to connect both with God and with the entire community.

Fourth, Judaism is not unattainable for the lifestyle of "overworked Americans." Judaism rejects the stereotype that it must occur on an "all or nothing" basis. On the contrary, Judaism offers a *ladder of commitment*. We must strive to ascend this ladder, one step, one commitment, at a time. Even modest increments in Jewishness will have an impact upon us and our family, our relationship to God and to the Jewish community.

In each of these four cases, just as acculturation offers a synthesis between isolation and assimilation, Judaism provides for us a middle point between the wisdom of the past—of tradition—and the demands of the present. Once we feel comfortable with such syntheses, we can better approach our children.

In other words, as long as we are evolving as Jews, we will be able to advocate Jewish activities and commitments to our youngsters. Then we will wholeheartedly read Jewish books to them, speak of Jewish concerns at the dinner table, practice Jewish rituals with love, experience our views about God and prayer. In sum, we will model Jewish living as a cherished and natural way of life.

7. How shall we pursue the goal of making our child into a good Jew, a mensch?

Judaism has a great deal of wisdom and guidance for every aspect of our life. It is not confined within the walls of the synagogue but is easily available to assist parents in reinforcing the ethical values they seek to impart to the next generation.

Within this large corpus of Jewish "value concepts" are

- *tikkun olam* — to make a better world
- *kibbud av ve'eim* — to honor/respect parents
- *hiddur p'nei z'kenim* — to show respect for the elderly
- *rodef shalom* — to pursue peace among individuals and nations
- *lashon hara* — to not gossip or spread slander
- *zakhor* — remember the Holocaust to prevent such repetition
- *mishpakhah* — centrality of family
- *pikuah nefesh* — to save a life takes precedence above all
- *tzorkei tzibbur* — to assist in meeting communal needs
- *dan lekaf zekhut* — to give others the benefit of the doubt

Jonathan might object to joining the family in going to visit elderly Aunt Sadie, who is recuperating from hip surgery. He might claim it will be "boring." As an answer, you can say: "Judaism teaches us to act like a *mensch*. One way we do this is *bikkur holim*; we visit people who are sick. We believe that such visits are like medicine in helping the patient to recover."

Or Rachel complains about your invitation to a Russian Jewish family for *Shabbat* dinner, saying: "They are hard to understand, and they don't have kids my age." Use this opportunity to say: "Judaism teaches us how to be a *mensch*, and part of that teaching includes *hakhnasat orhim*, greeting newcomers and guests to our home and community, helping them to feel comfortable in their new surroundings."

Similarly, mothers and fathers might prominently display a family *tzedakah* box and insist that each family member deposit something each week from their earnings or their allowances. If a child is unenthusiastic, remind him or her: "According to Judaism, a *mensch* always shares at least a portion of his or her possessions with people less fortunate."

And if a child finds a lost object and wants to keep this unexpected treasure, it is a superb moment to introduce the Jewish notion of *hashavat avedah* — returning lost objects to their rightful owner. Here, too, being a good Jew, a *mensch*, offers specific guidance as to how to respond to a morally challenging new situation.

Likewise, if you become aware that your child and friends are teasing another youngster, explain the Jewish prohibition against *malbim p'nei haverav* (causing embarrassment to someone else). A *mensch* should never behave in such fashion.

If parents frequently frame their moral guidance in a Jewish mold, this will have a deep impact on the Jewish identity of your children. For example, one profoundly effective way in which my wife's deep commitment to Jewishness was transmitted by her parents was their constant reference to *baala-batish* (what a *mensch* would do in a similar situation). Rita even wrote a paper in a college child-development course assessing the influence this moral compass had upon her view of ethics and of Jewish identity.

Keep in mind that in addition to speaking about Jewish values to our children, to truly educate a *mensch* parents must also act in a *menschlich* fashion. If you want your child to be a *mensch*, you must love others and show them compassion, caring, and concern. Your children will emulate what you do. They will not pay attention to what you say unless you are consistent with your behavior.

8. What kinds of hands-on activities add to my child's growing Jewish identity?

I'm glad that you wisely connected Jewish identity formation with hands-on activities. These involvements, in tandem with *Shabbat* and holidays, lifecycle events and ongoing Jewish celebrations, will create a Jewish rhythm for your family. Children will not learn by words alone. They will not be convinced by abstractions. They need specific, hands-on experience and rolemodeling to forge serious bonds with Judaism.

> A strong Jewish self-identity is not achieved by merely telling the child "you are Jewish" and then letting him wonder in what way he is different from people who are not Jewish. [It requires] seeing and doing those things that are decidedly Jewish in character. . . . [Concrete] Jewish associations must provide warm and happy memories, to which there must later be added feeling about the worth and importance of Jewish life. (Hayim Halevy Donin, *To Raise a Jewish Child*, cited in Lena Romanoff, *Your People, My People*, pp. 121–122)

Hands-on activities commence the building of lasting Jewish memories that instill in your child affection for the joys of being Jewish. Gradually, as our sons and daughters mature, it is hoped that these associations will be joined by additional, age-appropriate connections. This will best create a positive sense of Jewish belonging.

At her *bat mitzvah*, a 13-year-old at my synagogue, raised with these building blocks to Jewish self-esteem in her toddler and elementary school years, reflected about taking such memories into Jewish adulthood:

> Why are people teaching their children to be Jewish and keeping the chain of Judaism alive? I know I will, because being Jewish is and always has been a big and wonderful part of my life. . . . I

remember when I was younger, I loved getting dressed up and going to *shul* on *Shabbat*. When it was time in the service for *Adon Olam*, my friends and I all ran up to the *bimah* and led the prayer. . . .

When I get older and have children, I'm going to teach them about being Jewish and let my children have magnificent Jewish happenings in their lives too. For I love being a Jew, and I'm going to keep *my* covenant with God and extend the chain of our Jewish heritage.

There are numerous activities that create opportunities for joy, pride, and positive Jewish memories with your children:

- cooking Jewish foods;

- practicing traditional, child-oriented Jewish rituals, such as *Shabbat* blessing of children and searching for the *hametz* on the night before Passover;

- participating in Jewish communal experiences, such as marching in the Israel Day parade;

- singing Jewish lullabies and songs;

- using vivid Jewish ritual objects, such as the *shofar*, Purim *graggers*, Passover *seder* plate, and *Kiddush* cup;

- engaging in Judaica arts and crafts—decorating a family or synagogue *sukkah*, creating *Shabbat* table objects, knitting a *kippah*;

- playing with Jewish educational games and toys, and collecting Israeli stamps and coins;

- creating a family video and photograph record of significant Jewish moments and milestones in the life of your family, and developing a Jewish family tree.

9. Rabbi, does my child really "need" religion/synagogue after all?

Being part of a specific religious tradition offers a context in which to respond to childhood encounters with spirituality.

> "Mom, Sally next-door says that God makes babies."
> "Dad, on TV people who die always go to heaven."
> "My teacher taught us that God created the sky and the ground."

In this vein, I recommend Rabbi David J. Wolpe's excellent volume entitled *Explaining God to Children: A Jewish Perspective*. Rabbi Wolpe offers discussions and exercises to empower parents to instill within children a sense of awe, of mystery, of God's presence, and of the miraculous in the world. In addition, *Explaining God to Children* discusses the painful reality of death, of illness, of bad things happening in the world of children and their families. A religious framework gives boys and girls the spiritual strength to encounter life and continue to grow, to mature, to cope.

> We want to create a family atmosphere that has sacred moments and a feeling of warmth. We want to encourage our children to question and to search. We want to make sure they learn how important it is to be good and to feel that they matter.
>
> Religion can help in all these critical areas of growth. Belief in God affects self-esteem, and searching for God together can help draw a family close. (David Wolpe, *Explaining God to Children*, p. 2)

To those parents who are reluctant to broach God-talk with children because of their own religious doubts, Wolpe cautions that they are inadvertently diminishing their offsprings' ability to cultivate their spiritual selves:

> Children have very sensitive antennae. They pick up the discomfort of adults no matter how skillfully hidden. In time, children learn that to ask about God does not help; their parents do not

know how to answer. They will themselves grow up without the vocabulary to talk about God to their own children.

A spiritual education is as important to a full life as an intellectual and emotional education. . . . We need an attitude toward the ineffable, the world beyond what can be seen . . . forces in the world that are over and above us, and even within us. . . . What we believe about God greatly affects how we view ourselves, other people and our world. (David Wolpe, *Explaining God to Children*, pp. 3–4)

Jewish children benefit greatly if their family enables them to go beyond books alone and into the world of religious encounter. To do so, first of all, it is vitally important for your family to include spiritual practices in your home life. This can mean simply saying a blessing—*barukh attah Adonai*—before you eat, or upon reaching a holiday or milestone, or on seeing a gorgeous sight in nature. The uttering of a blessing, which takes only seconds, instills in the youngster an attitude of gratitude, an indispensable ingredient for being happy in one's life. As our sages reflected: "Who is truly wealthy? The person who finds happiness in their lot in life." Moreover, saying a simple blessing invokes God's presence in the life of the family. The *hasidim* teach: "Where is God? Wherever we allow Him to come into our lives."

Parents say that they do not want to impose religion upon their children. To best enable children to make informed choices about doing Jewish things, give them the maximum of rituals, Jewish education, holiday celebrations, synagogue experiences. Only when they have such knowledge and experience can they really choose. How can children who have never experienced a traditional *Shabbat*, never built a *sukkah*, never sung *Dayenu*, make a "choice" about whether they want it in their lives? Give your child as much as possible. A little Judaism is better than none. A lot of Judaism is better than a little. There are infinite gradations.

To give our sons and daughters maximum Jewish exposure requires our parental and communal determination. These are among those critically important life-decision choices you must make for your child. And your child must sense the nonnegotiable nature of this your commitment. Moreover, to link the forging of Jewish memories to family, peers, community leaders, and religious leaders, synagogue affiliation is important. A Jewish youngster's healthy religious-identity formation benefits immeasurably by your family's affiliation with a congregation, enabling the children to identify with a specific rabbi, cantor, religious educator, and so on. Join a synagogue as early as possible in your child's life experiences!

> [People join synagogues] because they are searching for a place to discover God and spirituality. They seek a common community of faith . . . a sense of spiritual rootedness, inspiration and peace. . . . [Some others] want to feel that they belong, to develop and nurture friendships and relationships with [coreligionists. Others join] . . . to have a place that will assist them in passing down the important values of Jewish life to their children. (Steven Carr Reuben, *Raising Jewish Children in a Contemporary World*, pp. 153–154)

Once you join a synagogue, plug your youngsters into the expanding array of children's religious services offered by many synagogues. These are user-friendly settings for the young. Do not be fearful that your child will resist this commitment on your part.

> Parents say, "If I insist upon my child going to services, or to partake in Jewish rituals, they will become alienated!". . .
> Rather than fearing the response of children, parents must provide clear values. And yes, kids will rebel; that is what they do. But they need something to rebel against. A parent's value system is like a pier. You must have something to push off against.

(Dennis Prager, "Raising a Jewish Child in a Christian Society," audiotape)

In most congregations across North America, programs are structured to encourage young children to be in *shul* either Friday night or *Shabbat* morning. These include Torah for Tots (ages 1–4), mini-minyan (ages 5–8), and family services for parents and children. Synagogues frequently also provide children's Simchat Torah, Purim, and Hanukkah services, as well as family services for Rosh Hashanah and Yom Kippur.

These religious moments build a sense of comfort for the children encountering sacred spaces in our synagogues, interacting with the Torah and with spiritual leaders. Moreover, a parent's validation of religious experiences helps reinforce the staying power of these skills and memories for children in their formative years.

> A child learns, acquires skills, and evolves his or her Jewish self-understanding in the context of ritual moments. The importance to the child of an adult sharing a moment of strange and magical words cannot be overestimated. . . . We, like our children . . . become participants in a sacramental act. . . . Our actions may speak more loudly to our children than our words. . . . [In this fashion] we are exposing our children to our Jewish selves. (Sharon Strassfeld and Kathy Green, eds., *The Jewish Family Book*, p. 59)

10. Rabbi, does Judaism contribute to my child's identity formation and sense of belonging?

Providing children with a specific religious affiliation can be important for personal identity formation. Judaism has much to contribute. It offers a sense of community and belonging–to a specific synagogue community, a common spiritual history, and an ancient religious civilization.

The Jewish religion gives born Jews and Jews by Choice a common religious heritage, values, traditions, rituals, stories, and jokes. It gives all of us an anchor in the world. In contrast, the avoidance of religion may create a void in emotional, psychological, and spiritual development. The following painful reflection is offered by the adult child of a home lacking a clear religious identity: "I felt alone in a very basic sense. I never felt I belonged."

Furthermore, being part of a religious minority, the self-esteem of American Jewish children must be reinforced. Children must learn that being Jewish is not simply okay but is also *special*. The child's pride in being a Jew needs to be nurtured with specific content with regard to the full range of Jewish experiences and priorities.

I have learned, in sessions with families in my own congregation, that parents and students feel proud when they:

- learn that Judaism was the first religion to believe in one God and that Judaism created a setting in which Christianity and Islam were able to rise.

- are taught about the Jewish basis for praiseworthy values: primacy of learning, centrality of family, tolerance, *tzedakah*, comforting the bereaved, etc.

- witness multigenerational ritual experiences such as candlelighting, the Passover *seder*, Yom Kippur services, and holiday meals.

- realize that the Jews were chosen by God to fulfill a special mission. We are commanded to keep alive the truth of God's existence and of God's standards of right and wrong. Being a *chosen people* with a mission does not mean we are "better" than others, but it does mean that we are unique, special, and blessed with this divine responsibility.

Parents have indicated to me during Jewish-awareness workshops that many facets of Judaism are not only sources of pride but also of joy. They point to aspects of *Yiddishkeit* as diverse as Jewish foods, music, museums, ritual objects, games, and vacations to Jewish sites in the United States and to Israel.

Israel offers additional sources of Jewish pride:

- We can be proud of the remarkable achievements of the Jewish state. In less than 50 years, Israel has made its desert bloom. People from all over the world are being taught by Israelis how to grow crops in dry soil, how to conserve water, and how to take the salt and harmful chemicals out of water.

- We can also be proud that Israel uniquely has rescued and welcomed hundreds of thousands of Jewish and non-Jewish refugees, including survivors of crises among Vietnam's "boat people," Jews from Ethiopia and Russia, and Moslems from Bosnia.

- Israel also has produced remarkable discoveries in medical technology and health care. Hadassah Hospital in Jerusalem is a source of healing to the entire Third World.

- Israel has preserved and offered safe access to holy sites sacred to Judaism, Christianity, and Islam, enhanced by amazing archeological excavations.

- Israeli scholars have produced an unprecedented flowering of religious scholarship, and Israelis set the world-leading pace in the per capita reading of books.

Jewish children can share parental pride in the disproportionately high number of Jews who have contributed to science, culture, and social welfare for the world. It is a special moment for Jews

> when Elie Wiesel wins the Nobel Peace Prize, or Isaac Bashevis Singer receives the Nobel for literature, or Betty Friedan is honored as the "founding mother" of modern feminism, or Natan Scharansky becomes the international symbol of the struggle for human rights and resistance to the oppression of totalitarian regimes, or Paul Simon brings 750,000 ecstatic fans to their feet singing with one voice "Bridge Over Troubled Water." (Steven Carr Reuben, *Raising Jewish Children in a Contemporary World*, p. 170)

Jewish pride and joy also should be transmitted to our youth with carefully selected Bible stories, rabbinic parables, tales of Jewish heroes, Judaica movies, and other age-appropriate materials recounting our unique Jewish heritage. Creating a passion for Jewish life will forge a likely desire of youngsters to re-create Jewishness in the homes they establish during their adult years.

11. What is the impact of enrolling my child in a program of formal Jewish education? And of informal Jewish settings?

All recent studies have confirmed the positive impact that formal Jewish education can have in transmitting Jewishness to children. Clearly, the earlier a child is enrolled and the more consecutive years of Jewish learning usually creates positive attitudes toward Jewish continuity. Sylvia Barack Fishman and Alice Goldstein at Brandeis University published research in 1993 entitled *When They Are Grown They Will Not Depart: Jewish Education and the Jewish Behavior of American Adults*, showing that formal Jewish education is positively related to ritual observance in the home, membership in Jewish organizations, giving to Jewish philanthropies, seeking out a Jewish milieu, marrying another Jew, and opposing mixed marriage.

It is important to seek suitable Jewish formal education from ages 5 to 17, beginning with a Jewish nursery school and continuing in kindergarten and elementary school years in a Solomon Schechter or other Jewish day school, or in a sequence of synagogue Sunday and religious schools, followed by Hebrew high school.

Some parents complain about their own days in Hebrew school or Jewish day school. However, begrudgingly they realize that, without years of formal Jewish education, they would never have acquired the religious knowledge to function as a Jewish adult. One of the parents of youngsters in a local synagogue Sunday school, for example, reflected to a study group:

> I never fully appreciated my Hebrew school education until I went off to college. In my program there were very few Jewish students and the Christian kids constantly asked me questions about Jewish rituals, holidays, and beliefs. Because I knew the answers, I felt proud and reaffirmed in my Jewishness. God forbid, how I would have felt if my knowledge had not been so strong.

Furthermore, current-day Jewish education is light years ahead of the quality of Jewish classrooms in the 1950s and 1960s. Indeed, the 1985 demographic and attitudinal survey of the UJA/Federation of our MetroWest, New Jersey, Jewish community revealed that nearly 80 percent of parents presently regard the quality of their children's Jewish day school or synagogue school experiences as either "good" or "excellent." Only 1 percent find these settings "poor" or "unacceptable."

We *know* that formal Jewish education is critically important for our children. Do not fall into the trap of asking your children whether they want to attend formal Jewish studies, any more than you would offer them choices about secular education. I am reminded of a public lecture by radio commentator Dennis Prager to a national UJA Young Leadership conference. Prager's brother, a physician and observant Jew, recently complained to their parents that he had never learned to play an instrument. In response, their father retorted: "We offered to give you piano lessons as a child. But you didn't want them." Hearing this, Dr. Prager quipped with regret: "And why did you listen to me?"

Similarly, do not leave to a child's whims the critical decisions of participating in Jewish communal and Jewish group activities such as Jewish day camps and overnight camps, youth groups, *tzedakah* projects, and JCC activities. I cannot overestimate the importance of giving your children, who are raised as a minority in a non-Jewish society, the opportunity to feel the warmth and comfort, the self-esteem and the pride of being part of Jewish endeavors with boys and girls their own age. The "informal education" transmitted in this fashion should become an indispensable part of your Jewish family life agenda.

12. What is meant by Jewish family education? Is this something that would be important for my family?

Recent data indicates that Jewish identity will best be developed among children whose entire nuclear family is part of the educational process. In other words, Jewish family education must be structured not as a luxury, but as a necessity. The client for Jewish learning and Jewish experiences must be *the entire family*.

In the immigrant Jewish family during the early decades of the century, Jewish family education did not have to be organized in a structured fashion.

> The home itself was the parents' classroom. The content of Jewish education offered therein revolved around the telling of family, tribal and national histories. . . . Each religious festival was imbued with [its own] special home ritual. Even the central life-cycle

experiences—birth, *bris*, wedding, death—usually took place in the home. (Ron Wolfson, *Jewish Family Education*, p. 2)

However, as the immigrants and their children pursued integration into American life, they adopted the cultural model of the United States, in which religious messages were transmitted primarily via the congregational school. This segmented approach was viable for Jews as long as children lived in close proximity to extended family and resided in a heavily Jewish neighborhood. Today, for most Jewish families, neither of these requirements is met.

As a result, Jewish children are learning Jewish content in settings that are divorced from their home lives. Judaism is not being reinforced by parents, siblings, or the household. "Children pick up parental convictions and beliefs, and where there are none, a vacuum is created that is readily filled by gurus and sects and cults [or by secularism]. . . . The school can teach dates, history, and geography, but not the language that penetrates the soul" (Harold Schulweis, "Inreach: Ways Toward Family Empowerment," pp. 195–196).Working as a family and a community, we must develop a strategy of meaningful encounters for our children with Judaism. Formal and informal opportunities abound.

Educator Susan Werk suggests that you continually point out what is Jewish about your community: Go to the kosher butcher and bakery. Visit the Jewish bookstore and JCC. Go on a kosher symbol hunt in the local supermarket.

Create a network of families pursuing similar goals of promoting Jewish continuity. Join a *havurah*, a cluster of 8 to 12 households who share your beliefs and interests. Invite families who seem receptive to this agenda to share *Shabbat* or holiday meals with your family.

Judaica enhancements should be implemented with the intent of establishing a Jewish "rhythm," of attaining a "critical mass" of Jewish living for our young.

What it comes down to for parents is to ask ourselves how much we care. If we care very much, our challenge is to try to build a *critical mass* of Judaism in our children's lives. . . .

Where we come out in level of observance is less important than that—by the choices we make—we show our children that we value, that we learn with and alongside them, that we bring Judaism into our homes, that we educate them Jewishly and that together we experience Shabbat and other festivals in the cycle of the Jewish year—the framework on which is hung the more than 3,000-year-old history of our people. (Suzanne Singer, "A 'Critical Mass' of Judaism May Prevent Intermarriage," p. 4)

5

Why Be Jewish?
What's the Gain, the Pride,
the Joy?

U ntil quite recently, we American Jews knew instinctively where we would grow up and approximately where we would live. We had a general idea of the types of career options open to us, the type of person we might marry. In short, the parameters of our lives were more or less established. Our futures, by and large, were set. The question "Why be Jewish?" was almost a nonquestion. Whether religious or not, we were Jews. That was a fact of life.

Today, in startling contrast, we live in a world of free choices. These choices include not merely an expanding number of ice cream flavors, television stations, and computer programs, but also places to live, persons to marry, careers to pursue. It is a world in which everything seems open to choice. Sociologist Peter Berger wrote in *The Heretical Imperative:* "The modern individual . . . must choose in innumerable situations of everyday life . . . [and] this necessity of choosing reaches into the areas of beliefs, values, and worldviews" (pp. 13-20).

In today's environment of multiple options, Jewish teens and young adults are asking: "Why be Jewish?" "What's in it for me? "What is there to be excited about, especially if I am not particularly religious at this stage of my life?" The 1990 National Jewish Population Survey indicates that hundreds of thousands of born Jews, when asked about their religious affiliation, responded: "Nothing." They have become, not Jews for Jesus or adherents of another ideology, but "Jews for Nothing," silently withdrawing from our ranks.

With so many Jews contemplating whether to remain within Judaism, we must take seriously and respond to the inquiry: "Why be Jewish? What's the gain?" Here I shall share reasons for personal excitement, joy, pride, and commitment in being Jewish. I shall do so in terms of two genres of finding meaning in one's life: meaning sought in self-fulfillment and meaning found in commitments to larger ideals such as God, family, a distinctive peoplehood, and the world at large. In total, seven Jewish approaches to finding meaning will be discussed. Separately and collectively they answer the question: "Why be Jewish?" Each perspective has resonated with meaning and significance for many Jews.

SELF-FULFILLMENT VIA JUDAISM

We are members of an American society, best characterized by personal freedom, by "not having other people's values, ideas, or styles of life forced upon [us]" (Robert Bellah et al., *Habits of the Heart*, p. 23). Personal freedom expresses itself in the quest for fame, sexual conquests, quality relationships, inner peace, popularity, career and financial achievements, material possessions, levels of learning, and so on. One's "human potential" is generally viewed independently of requirements of family, religion, community, or tradition. "The search for self-fulfillment expresses itself in . . . the need to 'keep growing,' the urge to express one's 'potentials,' to 'keep in touch with one's own true feelings,' to be recognized for 'one's self' as a 'real person' " (Daniel Yankelovich, *New Rules: Searching for Self-Fulfillment in a World Turned Upside Down*, p. xviii).

These desires are widespread among American Jews and Gentiles alike. Americans from every walk of life are eager "to find fuller self-expression and add a touch of adventure and grace to their lives" (Daniel Yankelovich, *New Rules*, p. 5). The influential psychologist A. A. Maslow has defined five levels of human needs. The fifth in his hierarchy is self-actualization (self-fulfillment). This need must be addressed in our discussion of "Why be Jewish?" Being Jewish offers many opportunities for self-actualization, providing a variety of modes for different types of people.

The historian Gershom Scholem has defined three categories of Jews in terms of Jewish identity and personal enrichment: Head Jews, Heart Jews, and Hand Jews. Head Jews are cerebral, finding meaning and fulfillment in the realm of books, ideas, and discussions. Heart Jews seek serenity via holiness, spirituality, ritual, and prayer as routes to intimacy with God. Hand Jews are best inspired by communal, political, or philanthropic acts—by deeds that transform the lives of individuals, society, or the doer.

The Jewish tradition speaks simultaneously to Heart, Hand, and Head aspects. Nevertheless, each Jew does have a dominant mode—whether intellectual, spiritual, or communal. The same person might manifest different facets at different stages of life, in varying contexts, and as his or her level of Jewish interest fluctuates. In seeking self-fulfillment within Judaism, our goal should be to sample and savor qualities that best meet our personal needs.

As reflected in Conservative Judaism's ideological statement *Emet VeEmunah*, each of us should endeavor to be a willing Jew, a serious Jew, a learning Jew, and a striving Jew. We should locate ourselves on an infinite symbolic pyramid, with the three sides serving as ladders of commitments. We ought to be striving to ascend the rungs of these ladders, moving toward

increasing levels of personal involvement, knowledge, practice, and meaning. By seeking to ascend the three symbolic
ladders of commitment—Head, Hand, and Heart—each of us
will grow in our behaving, believing, and belonging within
Judaism.

HEART JEWS—
SPIRITUALITY AND RITUAL EXPRESSION

Judaism's path to spirituality is particularly significant at this
time of widespread spiritual longings. The quest for meaning,
for finding a spiritual core, is expressed by Vice President Al
Gore in his best-seller *Earth in the Balance*:

> I have for several years now been engaged in an intensive search
> for truths about myself and my life; many other people I know are
> doing the same. More people than ever before are asking: Who are
> we? What is our purpose? There is indeed a spiritual crisis in
> modern civilization that seems to be based on an emptiness at its
> center and the absence of a larger spiritual purpose. (Albert Gore,
> Jr., *Earth in the Balance: Ecology and the Human Spirit*, p. 367)

For many of us—Head Jews and Hand Jews—this quest goes
unnoticed. We are like the deaf man in a hasidic parable who is
puzzled by the strange movements of people in a courtyard
because he does not hear the music to which they are dancing.
    Yet for many others, for Heart Jews, Al Gore is correct.
When we observe the incredible success of parapsychology,
holistic healing, and meditations, together with New Age
literature and tapes; when a feature film, entitled "Stranger
Among Us," lauding the spiritual dimension of Brooklyn's
hasidim, is a box-office success; something must be afoot.
Rabbi Harold Kushner, coming in contact with people during
his lecture tours throughout North America, has noted this

spiritual thirst. "[People are beginning to realize that] there is a kind of nourishment our souls crave, even as our bodies need the right foods, sunshine, and exercise. Without that spiritual nourishment, our souls remain stunted and underdeveloped" (*Who Needs God?* audiotape). What is this spiritual concern? And how does Judaism relate to the needs of Heart Jews?

Prayer can be an effective mode for fulfilling spiritual needs. But we must have patience. Peak moments in formal prayer come unexpectedly and require a momentary suppression of our ego. Jews habitually involved in prayer aspire for those rare sensations of immersion in a "prayerful mood." The Tanzer Rebbe was asked by his disciples how he prepares for his daily prayer. He answered: "I pray that I might be able to pray." The Rebbe pleads that he might attain peak moments in which "heaven and earth symbolically kiss" and then return to their distant realms.

Rabbi Lawrence Kushner's *God was in this PLACE and I, i did not know* describes the biblical patriarch Jacob, upon awakening from a divinely inspired dream, uttering: "God was in this place and I, I didn't know it." The repetition of the pronoun "I" implies that as long as the "I," Jacob's ego, gets in the way of spiritual illumination, true fulfillment is impeded. But once our obsession with ourselves recedes, as we deepen our immersion into prayer, unconsciously the realm of God opens wide.

On the holiday of Sukkot, for example, we are commanded to eat and to reside in the *sukkah* for seven days. The only valid exception is inclement weather. When we notice that it is raining, we may say the *Motzi* blessing and resume our meal inside our house. For the rabbinic tradition, this leniency can be understood to imply that while seeking spirituality in the *sukkah*, if we still notice rain causing us to get wet, if we are still attuned to *the self*, then we should return to our mundane dwellings. Awareness of our physical lives is a clear indication that we have not entered the spiritual realm.

In a similar fashion, Jewish legend tells of two Jews, Reuven and Shimon, privileged to be among the generation crossing the Reed Sea. They had experienced the miraculous Ten Plagues in Egypt and now the awesome parting of the waters. Nevertheless, all the way across the river bed, they persisted in *kvetching*. They complained that the ground was slippery. They were annoyed that other Israelites were pushing and shoving. They were perturbed by shortness of breath. Soon enough they reached the other side of the Sea. However, by the time their complaining ceased, they had missed the miracle, the incredible spiritual moment at hand. Reuven's and Shimon's chances to open their souls to God in prayer had been squandered by an obsession with the self. Their opportunity to be fulfilled for the moment as Heart Jews had been missed.

For prayer to be a route toward Jewish spirituality, we must move beyond our rational, analytical first level of awareness into the realm of our soul. When we repeat and repeat the same refrain on the High Holy Days, especially on Yom Kippur, we try to move beyond the rational side of our mental processing and into our spiritual, emotive, feeling side. It is that mode we are in when we meditate, when we light *Shabbat* candles, when we repetitively chant a hasidic melody. It is our a spiritual mode. It is available to Heart Jews via prayer.

I am always struck by the sense of awe, of mystery, on the faces of young children when they lead the *Havdalah* (ending of *Shabbat*) prayers on Saturday night. The youngsters who chant the prayers do not intellectualize about their meanings. They probably are not able to translate many of the Hebrew words. Yet their spirits are totally immersed in the prayerful mood, the dimmed lights overhead, the smell of the spice box, the flicker of the candle, and the cup of wine. Picasso remarked that "it has taken me 50 years to draw like a child." Abraham Joshua Heschel, too, pointed to the innate, unblemished spiritual gift of youngsters. Small boys and girls have not yet "learned" to feel embarrassed by genuine responses to the wonder of sacred words, of a beautiful sunset and the first three evening stars. Children still are dominated by spirituality. Judaism, in its prayers and in its rituals, offers a way back into that God-given mode.

Jewish spirituality also means learning how to view life differently. It teaches us to understand spiritual messages, to view the world through the lens of religion. Paraphrasing the words Rabbi Abraham Joshua Heschel taught to his students: "We do not step out of the world when we [have spiritual experiences] . . . we merely see the world in a different setting." For spiritual access, we need a point of view, a religious perspective, "religious spectacles." An eye surgeon once said to me: "Rabbi, a religious person does not need just excellent eyesight, but also superb vision."

The ultimate test for Moses in the Bible was not his defense of a Jew against a violent slave taskmaster, or his rescue of Jethro's daughters from abusive shepherds, but rather viewing a "burning bush that was not being consumed." In the arid desert, hundreds of bushes burn on a weekly basis. How could Moses have become aware that this bush was a miracle? To realize that the bush was not being consumed by its fire, Moses had to suspend his tasks as a shepherd. He had to be willing to become immersed in watching this part of nature. Moses had to demonstrate the ability to see the universe through the lens of religion and to see divinity at work. He had to respond to the mystery, the awe that most of us take for granted. He had to answer the call that Heschel speaks of as "God in search of Man."

To be fulfilled as a Heart Jew, religion asks us to take note of the miraculous in our lives. In a valuable parental primer called *Something More: Nurturing Your Child's Spiritual Growth*, author Jean Grasso Fitzpatrick recommends:

Set aside some quiet time to think of a miracle in your life today. Did a 3-year-old offer a playmate a lick of his ice cream cone? Have roses bloomed on the garden fence? Has a toddler's scraped knee healed? Did you and your child read a poem together, or hear some music, that touched your hearts? Think of a few such gifted moments you may have noticed in the past week (p. 55).

Sensitizing us to the miracles in our lives is precisely the purpose of Judaism's system of saying blessings (*"barukh attah . . ."*). *Brakhot* are intended to awaken us to holiness, to the spiritual in our everyday encounters.

At a workshop for clergy, Rabbi Elie Spitz distributed one raisin to each person. He urged us to take a moment to feel the raisin's texture, to note its unique colors, to smell its distinctive fragrance, to chew it, slowly sensing its crunchy nature, and then to recite the blessing of gratitude: *"Barukh Attah Adonai . . ."*("Blessed are You, O God, Ruler of the Universe, Who brings forth produce from the earth"). The exercise was intended to emphasize the Hebrew blessing's attitude of gratitude and appreciation of the miraculous qualities of God's creations. If we always could view nature through the lens of religion, our souls, not just our bodies, would be nourished. "[Judaism] is an inventory of moments in our lives in which we do and have things happen to us, in ways in which our eyes are opened to see God. God, in a world which can be so beautiful and so holy, so full of meaning and satisfaction, if we only opened our eyes to look" (Harold Kushner, *Who Needs God?* audiotape).

Involvement in Jewish prayer and its system of blessings can give us a sense of holiness, of contact with cosmic meaning. One Jew by Choice in my congregation observed:

This is precisely why [one] . . . converts, because of some sort of experience of something spiritual that has never been accessible prior to undertaking this perilous journey. A window was somehow miraculously opened. At the time of illumination the convert may be in awe as his whole disposition reflects the extraordinary process of transformation going on within . . . the power of God at work.

If you are a Heart Jew, in search of spiritual satisfaction, carefully investigate Judaism, its meditative prayers, its parables and sacred wisdom literature. Heart Jews can also be inspired spiritually by Jewish rituals. These holy acts have their own intrinsic value. There is a spiritual power in a Jewish life that puts us in touch with the Ultimate, with God. Judaism sanctifies life. Unlike some other spiritual modes, Judaism does not seek to remove us from other aspects of life. We need not adopt a life of celibacy or separate ourselves from our families.

Life structured by Jewish ritual can be self-fulfilling. Jewish ritual offers a meaningful process for dealing with emotion-laden points in our lives. Many of us have witnessed the healing power of a house of *shivah*, mourning the loss of a loved one. One local outreach worker of our Jewish Family Services had continually articulated the psychological value of Judaism to clients. However, only after experiencing Jewish mourning practices firsthand did she truly comprehend the power of this message. Soon after the death of her father, this woman said to me: "Only now did the total therapeutic impact of the Jewish response to death become a reality for me."

Other Jews have been equally moved by the awesome transitional moments of bestowing a Jewish name upon an infant male at the *bris* or upon an infant female during the baby-naming at synagogue. These celebratory formulas for rejoicing at a birth mirror the world around us. They reflect participation both in the miracle of creation and in the formation of the newest link in the Jewish tradition, spanning centuries. Equally moving for many Jews is the religious pageantry shared under a Jewish wedding canopy (*huppah*), sanctifying marriage. Moreover, Judaism provides a rich medley of holidays, with emotions ranging from the serious introspection of Yom Kippur to the hilarity of Purim and the home hospitality of Passover. "Marriage ceremonies, funerals and mourning customs [as well as *bar/bat mitzvah*, *bris* and baby-namings] are all ways religion gives us of taking a private event and giving it public expression, so that we are not left alone on those emotional mountain peaks" (Harold Kushner, *Who Needs God?* pp. 104–105). "Ritual is food to the spiritually hungry. Ritual has the potential to heal and warm; to glorify God and reify human devotion; to make objects and places sacred; to create community" (Letty Cottin Pogrebin, *Deborah, Golda and Me*, p. 56).

We should not allow our rituals and Jewish laws to be a source of awkwardness to us, but rather a source of pride. Many Jewish parents cringe at explaining to their young children why we do not celebrate Christmas. What they neglect to point out to their children is what we do have. In the winter of 1983, at age 3, my son asked me that inevitable question, "Dad, why don't we celebrate Christmas?" I answered, "David, Christmas is a terrific holiday for Christian people, but if we were Christians we would not have all of our special Jewish holidays." I listed the holidays and my child immediately perceived that Jews are not impoverished in ritual life. Our calendar is filled with an elaborate array of holidays with rituals that provide a context of interpersonal emotional and spiritual health.

I vividly recollect my initial years as an undergraduate when I was not observant. As a type-A personality I studied around the clock each semester for fourteen consecutive weeks. I would take final exams and then, totally exhausted, return home for recuperation. There was no rhythm to my life, no pacing of energies. Each day and each night were interchangeable. All of this tedium ended once *Shabbat* entered into my life. Every seventh day I was mandated to break the frantic pace of my activities and allow my physical and spiritual self to be regenerated. In the words of Abraham Joshua Heschel, the Sabbath offered to me "holiness in time" (Abraham Joshua

Heschel, *The Sabbath*, p. 82). It provided a weekly 25-hour sacred window of escape. On *Shabbat* I could not do errands or finish tasks; I could not keep myself glued to the telephone, the typewriter, and other addictive technologies; and I could not roam far from home or from the *Shabbat* dinner table. As one of my congregants reflected: "On Monday morning, when I get hassled at work, I simply begin the countdown to *Shabbat*." *Shabbat* offers a special pace for our lives. Conversely, the absence of ritual creates a terrible void.

> If one abandoned the synagogue, the High Holy Days, the Sabbath Queen, the Torah, the Talmud, the Midrash, what replacements are made in the building of the soul? How are the crises of life marked: birth, marriage, death? How are festivals managed? . . . What do we do—we who once thought only of abandoning the ways of our parents and parents' parents and gave no heed to necessary replacements, substitutes, we would need to make—what do we in our empty apartments do to make furniture and fabric for ourselves? (Anne Roiphe, *Generation Without Memory*, p. 18)

Judaism's prayers and rituals offer religiously satisfying opportunities for Heart Jews. For those who delve seriously into our rich legacy of teaching and observances, Judaism opens a sanctified view of the world. In *The Search for God at Harvard*, *New York Times* writer Ari Goldman observed: "[For me Jewish spirituality] makes everything holy, ties me back to history and connects me with the spirit of God" (p. 45).

Another powerful dimension of Jewish spirituality relates to Jews in recovery from addictions (to alcohol, to drugs, to food) through the 12-Step programs. It was my privilege for several years at my synagogue to host a group for Jews in Recovery. In this setting, I heard the following apocryphal tale of a rabbi who turned to his congregation on Yom Kippur, just before *Al Het* (the confessions of our sins). He told them he wanted to give a sermon about the addiction to lying. The rabbi proceeded to ask those assembled: "How many of you have read

the chapter in the Book of Proverbs about lying and liars?"
Numerous hands went up. "Good," he said, "you are just the
group I wanted to address. You see, there is no such chapter."

Recovery from harmful habits and addictions begins with
an end to denial, to lying to oneself. It teaches the 12-Step
process, with a recognition of our spiritual need. Recovery
commences with an acknowledgment that we might have
become powerless over habitual lying, over alcoholism, over
drug addictions, over unhealthy sexual relationships, over
excessive food intake, over squandering money, or over pro-
crastination. The program offers a way out of addiction. It does
so by teaching people to "work on their spirituality." Rabbi
Abraham Twerski, a pioneer in this field of recovery, has
commented: "Human beings differ from animals in that, beyond satisfying biological drives, we need spirituality, different people in different degrees. When spiritual needs [for
some] are not gratified, some people feel disoriented . . . [We
work on our spirituality] . . . to become the persons [we] are
capable of becoming" (Abraham Twerski, "Animals and Angels: Spirituality in Recovery," videotape).

Heart Jews, seeking sobriety and spiritual succor in Alco-
holics Anonymous, Overeaters Anonymous, or the plethora
of other recovery groups, often have questioned whether this
approach is consistent with Judaism. They ask: "Rabbi, what
does Judaism have to offer to those of us in recovery, seeking to
work on our spirituality?" Rabbi Neil Gillman, the foremost
theologian of Conservative Judaism, has indicated that the 12-
Step program is very much in harmony with aspects of Judaism. It bears many similarities to Maimonides' classic descrip-
tion of the steps necessary for *teshuvah* (sincere repentance),
for "turning one's life around" to a new path.

In the first of the 12 steps, as in *teshuvah*, we must acknowledge our powerlessness over the addiction and our need for
change. This is what Maimonides called *hakarat ha-het* (the
acknowledgment of the sin). We must sense our impotence,

that we have reached the depths. It is time for the death of our old self and of birth anew. As our next step, we must accept the existence of a "higher power," God, who is both our Father (merciful) and our King (just). We need to place our total dependence upon God, the all-powerful Creator of Heaven and Earth. As a third step for recovery and for *teshuvah*, we need to feel remorse, *haratah*, for any harm caused to ourselves, our loved ones, and our acquaintances. The next step is expressed in *vidui*, our confession. As in the repetitions of the Yom Kippur prayers, there is something therapeutic and spiritually cleansing evoked by verbalizing our shortcomings. It is equivalent to when a parent insists that a child say, "I'm sorry." Mother and Father are not just being stubborn; rather, they realize that it is a transformative act. People need this spiritual release.

In addition, as in 12 Steps, *teshuvah* requires that we apologize to those whom we have harmed, whether intentionally or unintentionally. We are enjoined to recite the following formula: "If I in any way have either intentionally or unintentionally offended you, I apologize and seek your forgiveness." I would also add the following corollary, suggested by one of my congregants: "I also express appreciation for all that you have done for me during the past year." Furthermore, *teshuvah*, like 12 Steps, insists upon a "New Year's resolution," *kabbalah le'atid*, to do better in the year ahead. Finally, 12 Steps and *teshuvah* require *azivah*, that is, transforming our behavior when the same situation arises. For Judaism and for 12 Steps, "working on our spirituality" is a remedy to bringing us back into contact with our true selves.

HAND JEWS—
ASSISTING FELLOW JEWS AND SOCIAL ACTIVISM

Some Jews do not relate to their Judaism primarily through the spiritual dimension of their lives. If they are Hand Jews, self-fulfillment might best be achieved via religion in action—helping one's fellow human beings.

Judaism offers a hands-on sense of community, an opportunity to assist and to interact with one's fellow Jews. Jews can be involved in or helped by the diverse institutional world of synagogues and Jewish organizations—B'nai B'rith, National Council of Jewish Women, ORT, American Jewish Committee, and Jewish Federation agencies such as Jewish family service, Jewish vocational service, and Jewish homes for the aged.

Whether aid is needed for Jews overseas or those in our local Jewish communities, we are committed to helping one another. We offer our skills in Jewish cooking, in Judaica crafts, our expertise via committee work, and *tzedakah* in the form of monetary contributions. Whenever I ask Christian clergy what they admire most about Jews, they never fail to comment: "The remarkable willingness of Jews to come to the aid of one another." In 1992, more dollars were contributed nationally to the United Jewish Appeal (UJA) than to any other philanthropic cause including the Salvation Army, the United Way, and Catholic Charities, although Jews comprise less than 2.5 percent of the American population.

Something special can be said about persons who opt to spend their limited spare time at committee meetings of synagogues, Sisterhoods, Men's Clubs, and Federations in lieu of a card game, bowling, or tennis. Let no one ever feel that he or she is not a "good Jew," if his or her commitment to God and the Jewish people is primarily in direct service to the institutions of Jewish life. Synagogue officers, chairpeople, and other lay leaders are to be accorded an honorable place on the ladders of Jewish commitments. Similarly, there is something sacred about individuals willing to contribute meaningfully from their wealth to maintain congregations, Israel, and Federation agency projects. For Jewry, *tzedakah*, giving of time and/or money, does not mean "charity"—an outpouring of one's heart—but rather "righteousness," expressing with our hands what God wants us to do among our fellow human beings. Jews who are *ba'alei tzedakah*, who contribute money and/or their time, are exemplary hands-on Jews.

Hand Jews can also be religious enablers. These people feel closer to God by enabling others to observe Jewish holidays in a traditional fashion. My mother-in-law, for example, is an unusually outstanding cook and baker. She provides delicious Eastern European delicacies for Passover, for the High Holy Days, and for other sacred occasions. Many other exceptional Jewish men and women preserve the flavors and memories of Ashkenazic and Sephardic Jewry via recipes, fragrances, and aromas.

Other Hand Jews express themselves via Jewish crafts and artistry. Some congregational sanctuaries are adorned, for instance, by magnificent ark covers, embroidered by persons from the community. At our synagogue one gentleman, in particular, displayed extraordinary "hands-on" dedication. Among his many contributions, he designed and constructed a High Holy Day Ark, a smaller replica of our permanent ark. He joined another temple member to create a magnificent stained-glass window arrangement for our chapel.

Hand Jews also express their commitments via a connectedness to other Jews in need. I recollect the remarkable efforts of members of our congregation and of so many other congregations in "adopting" Russian Jewish families. Adoption meant meeting the newcomers at the airport; transporting them to apartments that had been stocked with food, linens, and other basic necessities; and connecting these immigrants with Jewish agencies for assistance in learning English and locating employment and health care.

Devoted Hand Jews are available to help others in need. They aid families in setting up and maintaining a house of *shivah* after a death. They are ready to coordinate the providing of meals for the mourners, to cover mirrors, and to prepare a basin of water for washing hands after the funeral. They provide support groups for divorced persons, single parents, new mothers, Jews in Recovery, and other clusters formed as the need arises. These wonderful Hand Jews are religiously motivated to visit and assist shut-ins, the elderly, and persons recuperating from surgery.

Jewish youth, too, have been motivated to respond as Hand Jews. I recollect one young woman, celebrating becoming a *bat mitzvah*, who was outraged by the death of a child in her town caused by the negligence of a driver under the influence of alcohol. The youngster used part of her monetary gifts to purchase video equipment for local police to facilitate the arrest and conviction of drunken drivers. Another young woman, whose mother has been suffering for years with complex illnesses, used the occasion of becoming *bat mitzvah* to launch an international pen-pal support network of boys and girls whose parents are struggling with disease. Thirty-three of our religious school children raised funds to assist a family of Righteous Gentiles, Yonas and Stase Ruzgias—non-Jews who risked their lives during the Holocaust to save endangered Jews and were now impoverished in Vilnius, Russia.

I vividly remember many hands-on experiences in my Jewish life. Notably, there was one during my first year in Caldwell, New Jersey. I was contacted by our Jewish Federation's Chaplaincy Office to bring Passover greetings to the six Jewish elderly, long-term residents of a state psychiatric institution. In fulfilling this imperative of *ahavat yisrael*—love for one's fellow Jew—I brought *matzah* and other holiday items to this isolated hospital setting. Five of the residents were unable to speak and showed no awareness of my presence. I felt discouraged. The sixth person, however, provided me with an unforgettable moment of holiness, of fulfilling the commandment of *bikkur holim*, visiting the sick. I was told that this woman was 85, received no family visits, and had not uttered a word for 30 years. When I entered the room and presented her with the Passover gifts, she suddenly opened her eyes wide, threw her arms around me, kissed me on the cheek, and said, *"Matzah, matzah."* Her holiday and mine had come alive. In the spirit of talmudic wisdom: A hands-on *mitzvah* had served as its own reward.

A by-product of the commitment of Hand Jews is a strong sense of community. If a Jewish person moving into a neighborhood seeks affiliation with the local congregation, the Jewish Community Center, United Jewish Appeal, or affiliates of national Jewish organizations, a networking process begins. Friendships, acquaintances, a sense of belonging, a planting of roots, and the availability of assistance via Jewish agencies are often the results. The interconnectedness among Jews offers a powerful sense of personal identity. Judaism tells a person who he or she is and from where they came. It links Jewish people to other Jews throughout the world. We sense this bonding every time we travel, seeking fellow Jews in American cities or when touring abroad. Los Angeles radio personality Dennis Prager has written: "Judaism . . . provides the sense of community and belonging for which Judaism is uniquely known . . . the instant intimacy that I have experienced with fellow Jews in Morocco, the Soviet Union and elsewhere throughout the world" (Dennis Prager, "Why I Am a Jew: The Case for a Religious Life," p. 27).

Prominent Jews have testified to their indebtedness to Jewish collective memory for their Jewish identity and values. The founder of modern psychology, Sigmund Freud, in a speech to the B'nai B'rith in 1926, observed: "Plenty of . . . things . . . make the attraction of Jews and Jewry irresistible – many obscure emotional forces, which were the more powerful the less they could be expressed in words, as well as a clear consciousness of inner identity" (cited in Anne Roiphe, *Generation Without Memory*, pp. 179–180). In his best-seller, *Chutzpah*, Boston attorney Alan Dershowitz commented: "My Jewishness is a very important part of my life. Indeed, though I live and participate quite actively in the secular world, my Jewishness is always with me, both consciously and unconsciously" (Alan Dershowitz, *Chutzpah*, pp. 10–11). The memoirs of New York's former mayor Ed Koch also reflect the power of Jewish identity: "As a boy . . . my world ticked to the beat of the Sabbath and Jewish holidays. It was more than a religion, it was a way of life, a way of looking at the world. It invested me with an unshakable sense of who I was" (Edward I. Koch, *Citizen Koch*, p. 10).

A hands-on approach to Jewish identity can lead to involvement with Jewish communal affairs and to benevolent interactions with society at large. Judaism is committed to the mending of the world and insists that humankind must not be content with the imperfections in the world. We are mandated to be God's partners in restoring the human condition to its initial state of perfection. Journalist Yosef Abramowitz has observed: "Why be Jewish? . . . Imagine what the world would look like if everyone valued human life. Imagine a time when justice prevails for all and there is peace. These are messianic images, and the Jewish system of life and *mitzvot* is a framework to bring us closer to this vision" (Yosef Abramovitz, "Why Be Jewish?" p. 47). Reform, Conservative, Reconstructionist, and Orthodox Jewish groups all are in agreement about this moral imperative, evident in Conservative Judaism's ideological platform, *Emet Ve-Emunah*:

> The [biblical] Prophets fought vigorously against any attempt to limit Jewish faith to the sacral or cultic domain. While not denying the beauty and significance of Jewish ritual, they also pointed to the world outside and to God's demand that we carry our faith beyond the Temple and to incorporate it in our relationships with our fellow human beings. Our imperative was clear: "Justice, justice shall you pursue" (Deuteronomy 16:20). The Prophets never tired of calling on us to loose the bonds of the oppressed, to feed the hungry, clothe the naked, and shelter the homeless. . . .

Their vision was that of the just and humane society intended by God as the goal of creation. . . . There is an unfinished agenda before us: *le-takken olam be-malchut haddai,* "to mend and improve the world under God's Kingship." (Robert Gordis et al., *Emet Ve-Emunah: Statement of Principles of Conservative Judaism,* pp. 44–46)

Author, philosopher, and Holocaust survivor, Elie Wiesel, has commented: "A Jew cannot remain indifferent to human suffering, whether in former Yugoslavia, in Somalia or in our own cities and towns. The mission of the Jewish people has never been to make the world more Jewish, but to make it more human" (American Jewish Committee advertisement in the *New York Times,* September 27, 1992). In addition to advocacy efforts on behalf of Jewish causes, American Jews have established many organizations to serve universal human needs.

Jews also have been disproportionately prominent in nonsectarian struggles for equality, compassion, and human dignity. In the evaluation of Rabbi Daniel Gordis:

It would not be fair, of course, to suggest that socialism, feminism or other similar political movements are Jewish movements. Many crucial contributions to these movements have been made by non-Jewish men and women. But at the forefront of each of these movements were Jews who, whatever their level of commitment to Jewish life and community, seem to have been profoundly influenced by their Jewish roots. Could this be the fulfillment of Isaiah's dream that Jews would serve as . . . a covenantal community which acts as a model for the other nations? (Daniel Gordis, *Am Kadosh: Celebrating Our Uniqueness,* p. 48)

Most parts of the Hebrew Bible echo the sentiment of the Psalmist, "Those who love God, hate evil." Biblical ideals of social justice constantly remind us of being slaves in Egypt. The memory of bondage has a sobering effect. It sensitizes Jews to the vulnerability of orphans, widows, and other impoverished or dependent persons. "Do not undermine justice for the stranger, the orphan, and do not take the widow's garment as a pawn. Rather, remember that you were a slave in the land of Egypt, and that the Lord your God rescued you from there; therefore do I command you to perform this directive" (Amos 2:7; Isaiah 10:2).

We Jews are enjoined to be a "light unto the nations," bringing God's standards of justice and morality to the interpersonal and international realms. Whatever political philosophy the Jew chooses, liberalism or conservatism, the individual Jew is commanded to be committed to the mending of society. We best can achieve this goal of social justice by acting not only as individuals but also as part of a sacred people sharing this quest. "If we act as individuals, our lives would be too short and the extent of our influence too small to effect much toward . . . righteousness on earth. But acting cooperatively, through [our] historic groups that have a longer life and a wider range of activity than any individual, we can each of us render service [to this transformative goal]" (Sidney Greenberg, ed., *A Modern Treasury of Jewish Thoughts*, pp. 49–50).

HEAD JEWS—RELIGIOUS BELIEFS AND INTELLECTUAL STRIVINGS

Perhaps you are a Head Jew. Perhaps you relate to life primarily not through prayer or ritual acts but rather through ideas, thoughts, and concepts. Judaism has been well known throughout the ages for advocating study, education, reading, discussion, inquiry, and grappling with ideas. We are a learned tradition, the "People of the Book." Judaism is insistent that study of Torah, which can be understood as intellectual engagement with the full range of Jewish experience, can bring a person closer to God. For nearly 3,000 years, we have read our Torah, the sacred scroll, in a public setting rather than among a cloistered few, the clergy.

All Jews have been expected to spend some time in study. Our texts praise the *matmid*, the person who studies virtually all the time. Aspects of rabbinic literature regard all distractions from study as *bittul Torah*, diversions from encounter with the Divine. The greatest Jewish thinker, Maimonides, regarded inquiry into traditional Judaic writings and secular subjects as ultimate expressions of what God demands from us. For Maimonides, study was holier than prayer, more pious than ritual observance. Rabbinic midrash teaches: "If you wish to come to know Him [God] who by His word created the world, study [rabbinic texts]. . . . For by doing this you will come to know Him . . . and will cling to His ways" (*Sifre* Deuteronomy, *Ekev* 49). In Judaism, study is not merely an exercise of the brain; it is a spiritual act.

For a Head Jew, the Jewish religion offers beliefs with which to contemplate sanctity and holiness in our world. Judaism's tradition has much to nurture and challenge the modern thinker—ideas regarding heaven and hell, the fate of the soul after death, the messiah, sin and repentance, God's role in our lives, and revelation of the divine will. Judaism posits that human beings are born free, free of any "original sin." For Jews, there are no intermediaries between the believer and God. In Judaism, the divine preference is more for deed (acts of goodness) than for creed (beliefs). We regard human indiscretions not as the result of sinfulness but rather as *het*, "missing the mark." Persons are not inherently flawed when they err. Instead, we are like unskilled archers with poor technique in using the bows and arrows of living. We are in quest of *teshuvah*, "returning our aim" to the correct path.

We do not claim exclusive Jewish possession of salvation in God's hereafter. We echo the Bible's assertion that all races and creeds are descendants of Adam and Eve. Judaism posits that each ethical person (Jew or Gentile) has a portion in the world to come. Furthermore, we reject any bias against women or against men. Both sexes stem from the original Adam, initially a combination of male and female. In addition, age-old Jewish sources declare a concern for life. We affirm human-kind's "stewardship" over nature and our eternal concern for animal life. Our concept of the messiah does not concentrate on our personal salvation. Rather, Judaism emphasizes the potential of this chaotic world ultimately to reach a state of perfect peace and justice. Moreover, Jews insist upon a God-given impetus to engage in medical science. Being "made in God's image" means that men and women have the capacity for being "like the Almighty," correcting flaws within nature.

The Torah provides us with revolutionary moral innovations of eternal significance. Among them are:

Unlike ancient societies based upon slave labor, the Bible abolished slavery among Jews. A Jew who fell into debt did not become a slave. Instead he/she became an inden-tured servant. The Jewish servant possessed human rights, guarantees of equitable treatment, and a limita-tion upon the duration of servitude (Exodus 21:2; Levit-icus 25:39–52).

Jews were reminded of their experiences as "strangers" in Egypt, a foreign land. This humbling memory sensitized them to proper treatment of strangers in their midst (Ex-odus 23:9).

A code of sexual morality was mandated for the Jews. They were commanded to be "holy" in sex acts. They were to remain distinctive from the pagan cultic practices of the Egyptians and Canaanites around them (Leviticus 18:3ff).

A Jewish person was to behave with honesty in business, with correct weights, scales, and other suitable tools for the ethical conduct of affairs (Leviticus 19:35–36).

Jews were enjoined to be helpful to the poor. Interest was not to be charged for loans needed to feed, house, or clothe less fortunate members of the community (Levit-icus 25:35–38).

Special consideration was offered to the widow, to the orphan, and to dependent persons, such as the blind and
the deaf (Deuteronomy 16:11–12).

A Jewish farmer was to leave part of the crop for the poor to
glean, and provide for the support of community institutions (Deuteronomy 23:21–23).

"Murder" was to be forbidden under all circumstances.
"Killing" could be sanctioned in self-defense or in war-
time. In contrast, murder of the innocent or of the defen-
seless was never to be tolerated.

We also are blessed with a comprehensive system of Jewish
values whose wisdom is available through Jewish laws, parables, tales, and philosophical discussions.

Some of the prominent value concepts of the Jewish religion
are the following: We place a high priority upon comforting
the mourners (*nihum avelim*) after a death in a family. We are
committed to the *mitzvah* of visiting the sick (*bikkur holim*). We
are enjoined to bring joy to bride and groom (*lesame'ah hatan
vekallah*) at the sacred milestone of Jewish marriage. We are
warned to be careful with our speech, lest we engage in
slander (*lashon hara*), harming the speaker, the listener, and
certainly the person maligned. We are commanded to show
respect for the aged members of the community (*hiddur p'nei
z'kenim*) as a source of memory, of wisdom, of tradition. We are
encouraged to be active in the organizational life of our synagogues and Jewish and civic groups, to avoid separating ourselves from the community (*tzorkhei tzibbur*). We must return
lost objects to their rightful owners (*hashavat avedah*) and stay
away from falsely acquired possessions.

We are expected to be respectful to our parents (*kibbud av
ve'am*), whether or not we comply with their wishes. We ought to
rebuke persons who commit moral infractions (*hokhiah tokhiah*),
lest misdeeds become habitual. We should always seek to be the
peacemaker (*rodef shalom*) among friends, family members,

neighbors, congregants. We work on the Jewish assumption that a momentum can be created for either reconciliation or alienation. We ought to make whatever sacrifices are necessary to redeem captives or hostages (*pidyon shevuyim*) and to save human lives (*hatzalat nefashot*). We are enjoined to feel a special bond with our fellow Jews (*ahavat yisrael*) and to love humankind (*ahavat habriot*). We are commanded to give everyone the benefit of the doubt (*dan lekaf zekhut*) in forming evaluations of them.

Judaism realizes that it is human nature to mistreat other human beings and to enter into the manipulative mode Martin Buber called "I-It." "I-It" implies interacting with others only to exploit their qualities—physical attractiveness, wealth, intelligence, or social status. Judaism offers a value system of *mitzvot* to transform selfish inclinations into acts of "I-Thou"—treating human beings in a moral, caring fashion. "I-Thou" is a selfless meeting of two entire personalities, not just isolated personal qualities. Some persons, perhaps, can attain "I-Thou" relationships independent of organized religion. However, Judaism's life-enhancing value system both transforms us and passes values on to future generations.

Several years ago a Conservative rabbi was approached by a Jewish young man who boasted of achieving a level of "I-Thou" human interactions independent of *mitzvot*. The young person, son of a rabbi, claimed to have attained Judaism's ethical ideals of feeding the hungry, sheltering the poor, comforting the bereaved, and visiting the sick. "Of what value," he insisted, "is organized religion?" The rabbi responded in a twofold fashion. First, these moral deeds are the fulfillment of *mitzvot*. Second, without being part of an ongoing religious tradition, this righteous man would become a "cut flower." He would look morally beautiful but would be cut off from his ethical roots. He would risk not being able to lead his children and grandchildren down a similar path.

Judaism remains ever open to personal exploration, questioning, challenge, and investigation. It teaches that the pursuit of truth is equivalent to searching for the signature of God. No scientific theory, no archaeological discoveries or theories, no aspect of secular learning is off limits to us. Judaism has never been harmed by challenges, only by indifference.

It is our obligation not to stick our heads in the sand. Instead, we wish to structure interactions of Judaic ideas with the best concepts held by society. Out of the ensuing ideological dialogue, we derive new syntheses and vitality. Novelist Chaim Potok, for example, has shaped his fiction around "core-to-core culture conflict." In his nonfiction, Potok's history of the Jewish experience, entitled *Wanderings*, portrays Judaism's ability throughout the millennia to encounter the best of ideas available within the world.

For Head Jews, Judaism is a treasure chest of books, of issues, of opinions, of values, of striving for answers. Ongoing inquiries into Jewish religion are available in Jewish community newspapers as well as in a wide range of Jewish magazines and journals.

Jewish religious ideas face the challenges posed by technology and by ever-changing societal mores. Based on Judaism's values and the work of learned scholars, Jews have guidance with regard to abortion, life-support systems, surrogate motherhood, genetic engineering, fertility medication, test-tube babies, organ transplants, autopsies, and the permissible limits of human sexual behavior.

Ours is a religious history filled with inspiring ideologies — Zionism as a powerful force in modern Jewish history, the collective vigilance against anti-Semitism, feminism in Judaism. Reform, Conservative, Orthodox, and Reconstructionist Jewries all offer views to be investigated by Head Jews in books and published reports, historical analyses and theological pronouncements. (For a list of reference books, please see Appendix III: Resource Guide.)

As an undergraduate at Cornell University, it was my encounter with Jewish studies that triggered my involvement in

Jewish religion and social action. As a Head Jew, books, ideas, and issues were the first line of appeal in my growth as a Jewish young adult. I was intrigued by reading Jewish history, assessing our people's interaction through the millennia with every major culture. It was incredible to learn historian Salo Baron's thesis that Jews under medieval Islam and Christendom lived better than 99.9 percent of non-Jews. Most Gentiles were the penniless serfs of feudal overlords and were denied education, the opportunity to travel, the prospect of a better fate for their children. In contrast, many Jews lived unattached to the soil and thus were eligible for commerce, for cultural contact, for learning. Jewish status became so lofty that laws were passed making conversion to Judaism illegal.

I was mesmerized by the range of issues addressed by Jewish philosophy classes: How can we believe in God if bad things happen to good people? Are we able to reconcile God's knowledge of future deeds with our free will to choose? I also was drawn to the dilemmas emerging from the Holocaust: Did Jews resist or were we passive, like "sheep led to the slaughter?" Why did world leaders refuse to intervene? To what extent did Gentiles risk their lives to save our brethren? What are the motivations of those groups who question the historicity of the Holocaust? How shall we pursue and prosecute Nazi war criminals? Ultimately, I began to find personal fulfillment in interacting with Jewish sacred texts.

Other Head Jews have been stimulated by Jewish studies courses on many campuses, the presence of Jewish titles at most bookstores, and the frequency of media attention to Jewish issues. Paraphrasing advice that Rabbi Louis Finkelstein, former chancellor of the Jewish Theological Seminary, used to tell his students: Physicians are equating longevity in life with physical exercise. They are only partially correct. The real secret (of octogenarian JTS scholars still producing seminal books and articles) is mental exercise, *talmud torah* (the study of Torah).

The Talmud records that the question was asked: "What is more meritorious, *talmud* (study) or *ma'aseh* (deeds)? Rabbi Tarfon said *ma'aseh*. Rabbi Akiba said *talmud*. They finally agreed that study takes precedence, for it motivates and induces good deeds" (Simon Greenberg, *A Jewish Philosophy and Pattern of Life*, p. 302).

Jewish devotion to learning, *keneged kulam*, "above all else," has brought countless persons closer to Judaism. The 1977 Nobel laureate Dr. Rosalyn Yalow reflected: "Throughout the ages, we have taken pride in being known as the 'People of the Book.' . . . The Jewish people, never satisfied with conventional answers, have always valued intellectual inquiry and continued to honor wisdom and learning" (American Jewish Committee advertisement in the *New York Times*, March 7, 1993).

The Jewish route to self-fulfillment via Torah study is described in Vanessa Ochs's personal memoir, *Words on Fire: One Woman's Journey into the Sacred*. Ms. Ochs chronicles her spiritual odyssey from disinterest to curiosity and then to passionate study of the Torah, its commentaries and existential issues. As a product of secular universities, she initially expressed reluctance: "I thought it would be boring. Hebrew school had been horribly tedious. Along with history and language, Torah was just another subject that only minimally engaged me" (p. 12). Beginning with a small study group of women, Ms. Ochs's interest was aroused. "Studying together, you develop a profound sense of personal intimacy. You open up spiritually to each other. If you're learning Torah seriously, you bring your whole being into it, share your deepest inner experiences . . . and become close personal friends" (pp. 93–94). As she read and discussed Jewish texts, Vanessa Ochs came to appreciate their transformative power. "The rushes I [now] get reading Torah . . . it's like falling in love . . . I feel so many associations reading the text . . . I have an overwhelming sense of returning home . . . to my place and people. . . . I reclaim a vital, missing part of myself" (p. 195).

Self-fulfillment via Judaism's intellectual tradition is more accessible than ever. There are thousands of English-language volumes, magazines, and newspapers with topics ranging from Jewish beliefs and values to Jewish history and lore, Bible and Talmud, Jewish literature and the arts, Jewish law and practice, as well as views of contemporary political, moral, and scientific concerns. Judaica courses for adults are offered by institutions of Jewish studies as well as at community centers. Judaica also is provided at many universities. Jewish museums, within most major metropolitan areas, offer Jewish art and public lectures.

For the Head Jew, as with the Heart Jew or the Hand Jew, Judaism includes an array of opportunities for self-fulfillment. Many Jews find their interaction with Judaism to be not primarily through prayer or ritual practice but rather through books, journals, ideas, and inquiry. Rabbi Finkelstein used to assert: "When I pray, I speak to God. When I study Judaism, God speaks to me."

To be a Jew is to be potentially enriched in many different ways. It is an inspiring religious system, yet it is more than involvement in Jewish rites and sacred symbols. Judaism also can involve the intellectual and the hands-on dimensions of our personalities. In none of these three domains—Heart, Hand, or Head—is Judaism all or nothing. Furthermore, Judaism offers commitments that transcend the self and connect us with larger ideals—to Jews throughout the ages, to Jews around the globe, to the world at large, and to God.

In 1979, social scientist Daniel Yankelovich identified a societal trend of seeking "an ethic of commitment" beyond simple self-gratification, beyond a "Yuppie lifestyle":

> The word "commitment" shifts the axis away from the self (either self-denial or self-fulfillment) toward connectedness with the world. The commitment may be to people, institutions, objects, beliefs, ideas, places, nature, projects, experiences, adventures

and callings. It discards the Maslowian checklist of inner needs and potentials of the self, and seeks instead the elusive freedom Arendt describes as the treasure people sometimes discover when they are free to join with others in shaping the tasks and shared meanings of their lives. (Daniel Yankelovich, *New Rules: Searching for Self-Fulfillment in a World Turned Upside Down*, p. 250)

Rabbi Harold Kushner's volume entitled *When All You've Ever Wanted Isn't Enough* offers the following analogy:

A rabbi once asked a prominent member of his congregation, "Whenever I see you, you're always in a hurry. Tell me, where are you running all the time?" The man answered, "I'm running . . . after fulfillment." The rabbi responded, "That's a good answer if you assume that all . . . blessings [are achieved in that fashion] . . . but isn't it possible that God [and family, and our ancestors, and the world] has all sorts of wonderful [meaning] . . . for us . . . but we in our pursuit of [fulfillment] . . . are so constantly [oriented toward seeking self-fulfillment] . . . that God [and family, and ancestors, and the world] can't find us [ready to be encountered]?" (p. 146)

In American life today, people are searching for community and for meaning. Judaism offers anchors to our identity via Torah, the covenant with God, and a system of *mitzvot*. The Jewish tradition asserts that to find meaning in life Jews must connect with transcendent values, institutions, the Jewish people, and God. Jewish lore suggests that the Ten Commandments and other laws given on Mount Sinai to Moses as *harut* (engraved in stone) were actually our source of *herut* (true freedom). True freedom comes about when a person makes a commitment to a discipline. It is analogous to a violin string that hangs loosely in its natural state, but gains the freedom to express a full range of notes and fulfill its destiny once it is tuned and disciplined by a musical system. Similarly, my

children become bored if we play tennis without rules, volley-
ing aimlessly, not keeping score, ignoring infractions. Once
rules are added to the game, excitement and meaning enter as
well. Music and sports need laws, commitment to standards
that convey meaning. So too with the human spirit. We are
blessed with opportunities for significant living through our
commitment to tradition, to Jews throughout the globe, to the
world, and to God. All of these potential commitments can
have a claim upon us and can add significance to our lives.

Finally, being Jewish is our destiny. The permanent departure from Judaism by an individual Jew is not so easy to
achieve. Although a Jew may decide to cast aside his or her
Judaism, he/she cannot predict how much *Yiddishkeit*, Jewish
sensibilities, lifestyle will mean in later life. A superficial rejection of one's Jewishness belies deeper, subconscious strivings
to remain true to one's real self. Author Anne Roiphe offered a
personal testimony to the persistence of Jewish identity: "[As a
young adult] I had thought that since I had removed God from
my life, the thin, watered-down Jewishness I had learned as a
child would wither and disappear. . . . The tree [of Judaism]
without its roots has surprised me with its staying power"
(Anne Roiphe, *Generation Without Memory*, p. 180).

Dramatic turnabouts with regard to Jewish identity are predicted by Jewish lore. Kabbalistic tradition teaches that even
alienated Jewish individuals still possess a *pintele yid*, a mystical spark of Jewishness. At times the spark burns at low ebb.
At other times, unpredictably, its flame begins to glow with
greater intensity.

A modern midrash on this theme is the autobiography of the
late Paul Cowan entitled *An Orphan in History*. Cowan chron-
icled his life as the son of a totally assimilated Jewish couple,
whose family name originally had been Cohen. As a child,
Cowan was never in a synagogue. He never went to Hebrew
school. He never had a *bar mitzvah*. He did not have Jewish
friends, and he attended Protestant private schools with afflu-

ent WASP classmates. Yet during his adult years a trip to Israel, the sudden death of his parents, meeting Jewish relatives for the first time at the funeral, and saying *Kaddish* collectively triggered Jewish identity within him. Our *pintele yid* cannot so easily be cast aside.

In a High Holy Day sermon in 1992, Rabbi Jeffrey Wohlberg of Washington, D.C., related an apocryphal episode in the life of Louis D. Brandeis:

> In his senior year of law school, his pre-eminence could not be denied. Jewish or not, he was invited to join the exclusive Honor Society. On the evening of the official induction, the atmosphere was thick. All eyes were on him as he walked to the lectern. Slowly, he looked around the room. "I'm sorry I was born a Jew," he said. The room erupted in applause, an explosion of shouting and cheers. They had prevailed upon him at last [to convert into Christianity]. Brandeis waited. When silence was regained he began again. "I am sorry I was born a Jew, but only because I wish I had the privilege of choosing Judaism on my own." This time there was no shouting, no explosion, no cheers, this time there was respectful silence. The members of the society were awed by his conviction and strength of character. When he finished they gave him a standing ovation. (Rabbinical Assembly Homiletics, 1992)

Given the enormous blessings Judaism can provide, do not forego such a heritage. Judaism has a rich and compelling legacy that speaks powerfully to us today, as it has to Jews throughout the ages.

Being Jewish is a multifaceted blessing. It is a source of pride and of joy. It enriches our lives in a variety of ways. In this age of unprecedented choices, be appreciative of your Jewishness. Do not take for granted this precious legacy and its ability to speak to you even today. Before you ignore or discard this incredible heritage, study it, savor it. It will enrich your life and the lives of those around you.

6

Looking Ahead

What does the future hold in store for us as Jews in America? American Jewish experts debate the prognosis for Jewish survival. Pessimists claim that the descendants of Eastern European Jews will eventually disappear as did most of the descendants of the 250,000 German Jews who came to the United States before 1880. Historian Arthur Hertzberg observed:

> Wherever freedom has existed for several generations without a break, the Jews have never in the last two centuries settled down to be themselves. . . . In the third and fourth generation it [the disappearance as Jews] began to approach one-half. Today in America we are reaching the stage of the great-grandchildren of the Russian Jewish immigrants of . . . a century ago, and all the indices of disintegration are beginning to arise. (Arthur Hertzberg, *Being Jewish in America*, p. 208)

In contrast, optimists have offered persuasive evidence for effective Jewish continuity. For example, at the 1993 convention of the Rabbinical Assembly, Professor Jonathan Sarna debunked the misguided prophecies of doom that perpetually cast a cloud over the Jewish future. Among Dr. Sarna's colorful examples was an infamous prediction by *Look* magazine in the 1960s proclaiming the disappearance of American Jewry by the 1990s. Yet today Jews are alive and well, while *Look* has long been removed from the scene.

Who is correct, the pessimists or the optimists? An insightful compromise was offered in an influential essay aptly entitled "American Jewry—The Ever-Dying People" by sociologist Marshall Sklare. Sklare noted the high rate of assimilation among those American Jews for whom Judaism was of marginal significance. Yet, at the same time, he pointed to a committed core of Jews in the United States who continually have beaten the odds by remaining pro-active on behalf of Jewish continuity.

Examples of the successes of this core group during the past 25 years include the following:

- The remarkable growth of Jewish day school enrollment in the 1970s, 1980s, and 1990s, including as many as 20 percent of the children of Conservative Jews.

- The resurgence of Orthodox Judaism, spreading to America's affluent suburbs, thereby defying the 1960s' predictions of doom.

- The spread of Judaic studies programs and course offerings to dozens of major American colleges and universities.

- The post-1967 burgeoning of Jewish Federations as major financial, educational, and ideological proponents of Jewish identity.

- The dramatic expansion of tourism, political activism, philanthropic activity, and identification of American Jews with the State of Israel.

- The sizable growth of multigenerational *Shabbat* morning attendance at many Orthodox and Conservative congregations, which offer parallel "Torah for tots," mini-*min-*

yan, family service, learners' *minyan*, and other options for prayer.

The issue addressed by this volume is: Once the Jewish concerns about interdating and intermarriage are known to us, what choices will we make in our lives? Will we choose to identify with the committed core group of American Jews, dedicated to preserving the blessing of our Jewish heritage for future family members? Or, by our inaction, will we permit the forces of assimilation in America's open society to erode the Jewish future of our families?

We should adopt an activist strategy to promote marriage by American Jews with one another. Although there are no guarantees, keep in mind the actions most likely to ensure that our sons and daughters marry one another:

- Be specific in clarifying your personal credo regarding why being Jewish is important, special, and a priority.

- Verbalize your concerns regarding interdating and intermarriage. Be certain that your children know where you stand. Be prepared to address their questions and challenges.

- Articulate Jewish values, Jewish role models and heroes, and other Jewish identity concerns as an ongoing commitment.

- Provide as many years as possible of formal Jewish education for your children from pre-school all the way through high school.

- Seek Jewish day camps and then Jewish overnight camping experiences for your youngsters.

- Plan to send your sons and daughters to Israel at least once during their teenage years, ideally in a six- to eight-week program designed for Jewish adolescents.

- Insist upon a college that has a substantial Jewish student population and offers a full range of opportunities for Jewish living.

- Join a synagogue as soon as feasible, and retain membership as a tangible demonstration of the importance of Jewish religious identification.

- Promote Jewish friendship patterns by involving your sons and daughters in Jewish youth group activities.

- Demonstrate that Jewish learning is a lifelong commitment by reading and discussing Jewish books, issues, and values at the dinner table.

- Grapple with a step-by-step, incremental approach to adding Jewish ritual observances into the life of your household.

- Develop a network of other Jewish families with children of similar ages with whom to share Jewish celebratory and commemorative occasions.

- Help single Jewish adults to connect with Jewish singles programs, retreats, conferences, and organizations.

American Jewish history has taught us the peril of inaction with regard to interdating and intermarriage. However, history also shows that energetic efforts to preserve Judaism for our future family members is both possible and effective. Read and reread the material in this volume. Share this book or the appropriate separable booklets (each chapter can be obtained individually) with sons, daughters, other relatives, friends, neighbors, and coworkers. Let us make a principled statement about our Jewish priorities and overcome past habits of inaction. Keep in mind the words in the title: *It All Begins with A Date—Jewish Concerns about Intermarriage.*

Appendix I

Judaism and Christianity Are Different

M any people have the vague idea that Judaism and Christianity are variations of the same theme—to believe in God and be a good person—and that perhaps they are interchangeable.

One of the unfortunate assumptions of American secular culture is precisely this mistaken equation of Judaism and Christianity, the "Judeo-Christian heritage," as being identical and interchangeable. This facile generalization leads many youngsters to feel comfortable in considering intermarriage later in life, since they incorrectly assume that their children can be raised meaningfully in both Jewish and Christian traditions. Little do they comprehend that such youngsters grow into adulthood either avoiding organized religion entirely or choosing some eastern or New Age alternative, lest they have to choose between Mom's or Dad's heritage.

Furthermore, Christian religious life differs from that of Judaism at virtually every significant moment. We have different ways of ritually responding to birth, adolescence, marriage, and death. Judaism and Christianity have mutually respectful but differing beliefs about the messiah, the afterlife, the permissibility of abortion and living wills, cremation and other fundamental concerns. It is wrong to assume that we can comfortably function in or simultaneously experience both.

The key differences between Judaism's and Christianity's approaches to life-cycle events and to holidays are discussed briefly.

A *BRIS* IS NOT A BAPTISM

There are fundamental differences in the theological assumptions that Judaism and some Christian communities hold about infants, and these are reflected in their ceremonies. Christian baptism assumes that babies are born blemished by the "original sin" of Adam and Eve and need to be cleansed. The *bris* (or *brit*) assumes that babies are born pure and are ready to enter into a covenant with God.

For Christians who believe that infants are born in a state of original sin, God "washes away" this sin through baptism (John C. McCollister [Lutheran], *The Christian Book of Why*, p. 51). In addition, Roman Catholics as well as those Protestant denominations practicing infant baptism regard it as an act of "incorporation," formal admission into its religious community. The Episcopal *Book of Common Prayer*, for example, states: "Baptism is the sacrament by which God adopts us as His children and makes us members of Christ's Body, the Church, and inheritors of the Kingdom of God" (Episcopal Church of America, *Book of Common Prayer*, p. 858). Similarly, "through baptism, Catholics are delivered from original sin . . . [and given] entrance into the fellowship of the church" (Alan Schreck, *Your Catholic Faith: A Question and Answer Catechism*, pp. 72–73).

For Catholics, Lutherans, Eastern Orthodox, Methodists, and Presbyterians, infant baptism is traced directly to the teachings of Jesus. It is a sacrament, a "visible, tangible, effective sign through which [Jesus] God . . . enters [one's] life, and draws [a person] . . . to Himself through His grace" (Alan Schreck, *Your Catholic Faith: A Question and Answer Catechism*, p. 70).

In Judaism, the *bris* brings the child into a formal relationship with the Jewish faith community. In contrast to baptism, however, a *bris* is not a cleansing of any inherited moral taint. Rather, it is a sign of a child's entry into a covenant with God, a

God who judges each of us solely in accordance with our own deeds—not those of Adam and Eve, our ancestors, our parents, our children, our neighbors, or our coreligionists. Rabbi Harold Schulweis eloquently observed:

> Circumcision is the initiation into the covenant with God and Abraham. The 8-day-old child carries no baggage of [original] sin with him into the world. He is no alien flung into the hands of demonic powers. . . . The Jewish child is born innocent, body and soul, created and sustained in God's image. He has no need to be saved because no Satan threatens him, no eternal damnation hovers over him. As a Jew he will be raised in a tradition that mandates him to save lives, not souls. (Harold Schulweis, "Peering into the Limbo of Judeo-Christian Beliefs," p. 242)

Jewish *bris* and Christian baptism are both very special. They represent incorporation, the formal entry, into a specific faith tradition. Each, in its own way, brings youngsters into separate and distinct religious communities, which means that *bris* and baptism are totally incompatible with each other. Rabbi Harold Schulweis has pointed out, "Circumcision and baptism are not a knife-or-water option, dramas of values. They affect our relationships to God, world, neighbor and self" (Harold Schulweis, "The Hyphen Between the Cross and the Star," p. 173). Each marks the entry into a specific Christian or spiritual Jewish path. You cannot meaningfully be admitted into both belief systems.

BAR/BAT MITZVAH IS NOT CHRISTIAN CONFIRMATION

For adolescents, both Judaism and Christianity have ceremonial milestones, *bar/bat mitzvah* and Catholic confirmation. Both ceremonies mark the formal entry of the child into the specific religious community. Both rituals are laden with declarations of loyalty by the young adult to the particular church or synagogue tradition that sponsors the occasion. (Christian confirmation should not be confused with Jewish "confirmation" in Reform and some Conservative congregations.)

For Catholics, the sacrament of confirmation, like baptism, is traceable to the life and teachings of Jesus. For mainline Protestants, while not a sacrament, the confirmation ceremony "confirms" the teenager's earlier baptismal vows. For both groups, confirmation is a ceremony of "incorporation," of final acceptance into the religious community of faithful Christians. It is "the 'bestowal,' through prayer and anointing, of a fuller empowerment of the baptized person by the Holy Spirit so that he or she may lead a fuller Christian life" (Alan Schreck, *Your Catholic Faith: A Question and Answer Catechism*, p. 75).

> [The sacrament of] confirmation is an affirmation of belief in a particular doctrine. The person is confirming the faith to which his [her] parents brought [him/her] at birth. The ceremony takes place during a Sunday service, with the individual making a personal statement or agreeing to a credal vow stated by the clergyperson.
>
> The confirmation is [usually] a group event. It takes place . . . generally about age 12 [or as late as age 16]. The ceremony conveys full membership in the congregation. (Judy Petsonk and Jim Remsen, *The Intermarriage Handbook*, p. 251)

Bar/bat mitzvah is similar to confirmation in that it too provides a ceremony of "incorporation," of formal entry into the Jewish community. It is usually a ceremony honoring one individual youngster; the exception is in very large congregations in which two or sometimes three honorees are involved. This entry into Jewish adulthood occurs over the reading of the Torah, Judaism's most sacred and self-defining possession. The 13-year-old boy or 12- or 13-year-old girl is reminded that he or she is becoming the newest link in a Jewish chain of tradition that spans centuries. Like Christian confirmation, this milestone is a public act of loyalty by a young adult to one specific religious community, to the exclusion of membership in any competing religious system of faith.

RESPONSES TO DEATH
IN JUDAISM AND CHRISTIANITY

Inevitably all of us will encounter the death of a loved one. It is important for a person reaching adulthood to have specific regimens of response to such times of emotional stress. Offspring do best when they have witnessed parents considering and deciding "what we do." Separate and contradictory sets of rules or a family pattern of indecisiveness will add to a person's grief and disorientation. For example, when a person raised in both religions dies, it is impossible for a sibling, also the child of intermarrieds, to approve of mausoleum (aboveground) burial, as in Christianity, and simultaneously to disapprove of it, as in traditional Judaism. It is impossible to bury one's relative almost immediately (Judaism) while delaying burial until after a vigil or a wake (Christianity). An open casket or viewing is common for many Christian groups, but it is forbidden for Jews. Kneeling in prayer and crossing oneself is proper etiquette in some Catholic and Protestant settings, yet it is totally alien to Jews. At the grave site, some Christians place flowers in the grave, while Jews place shovels of earth.

A separate yet related dilemma occurs at the time of a tragic death of a child of either no religious affiliation or of dual affiliation. Here too the intermarried family has one more painful decision to make. Should the son or daughter be buried in a Christian or a Jewish cemetery? Will the designated cemetery accept such an unaffiliated person? Will burial among Jews alone imply that this deceased youngster will not receive heavenly rewards in the eyes of a Christian parent? Will burial in a Christian setting be felt as an eternal betrayal of one's ancestors by a grieving Jewish parent? These unresolved latent concerns add enormous layers of complexity to an already traumatic situation. Moreover, life-and-death decisions may reawaken the intermarried parent's unresolved tensions regarding his or her religion of birth.

A SYNAGOGUE IS NOT CHURCH

Synagogue and church religious services reflect dramatically different theological assumptions. The Rev. Ronald Osbourne, a former chaplain at University of Iowa, observed:

> When Jews worship with Christians, almost nothing is accessible, almost everything is problematic. . . . "Old Testament" readings are selected in the Christian lectionaries to interpret New Testament experience. Even the Psalms gather Christian meanings. . . . [In addition] "New Testament" readings, creeds, prayers, trinitarian invocations, acclamations and doxologies, are all utterly impossible to a Jewish participant, or at least one with theological sensitivity and integrity. (Ronald Osbourne, "Marriage of Christians and Jews," pp. 9–11)

Moreover, church displays of Christian symbols, notably in Roman Catholicism, with the cross, and particularly the crucified body of Jesus, are irritating reminders to the Jew of the thousands of coreligionists who have died in the past at the hands of Christian mobs. Jews also are ill at ease with references to the Trinity, to Jesus as messiah, to Catholic overtones of sin and forgiveness, to the virgin birth, saints, celibacy for clergy, confession, kneeling, and to a spiritual distance between the laity and the status of priests, nuns, and other people "of the cloth." While mainline Protestant churches do not possess some of these features, their own clergy robes, communion rites, offerings, organ and choir-led hymns, absence of male head coverings, passing the plate, invoking the name of Jesus, bowing of heads, silent meditations, formality, and decorum are awkward for Jews.

Similarly, Christians need a reorientation to become comfortable with the synagogue service. Hebrew language is foreign to them, as is a prayer book that moves from right to left on the page, and from back to front within the volume. Ceremonial objects such as *kippot* (skullcaps), *tallitot* (prayer shawls), Torah scrolls, and private yet audible prayers are quite strange to the uninitiated. Newcomers might also be astonished at a synagogue's informality, its diminished reliance upon sermons, its lengthy liturgy, and its concentration in great detail upon the nuances of the sacred narratives in the Five Books of Moses. A person cannot "own" both of these religious services, let alone either one if treated superficially.

HANUKKAH IS NOT CHRISTMAS

Hanukkah and Christmas are more than empty shells for justifying exchanging presents or convening an extended family meal. Both holidays are expressions of religious values fundamental to Judaism and to Christianity, respectively. Christmas asserts that Jesus was born in order to replace the Torah as God's preferred route to salvation for human beings. Hanukkah offers the opposite message, insisting that Jews be willing to fight to preserve the unchallenged authority of the Torah.

Christmas is the spiritual reexperiencing of the hope personified in the birth of Jesus, with the intent of having the spirit of Jesus enter anew into the faith, the very being of the believing Christian. "[Protestant] Christians around the world celebrate Christmas as the birthday of their Lord,

Jesus Christ. The word 'Christmas' is a contraction of the phrase 'Christ's mass,' i.e., a service of worship honoring the Christ child" (John C. McCollister, *The Christian Book of Why*, p. 205).

"[For Catholics] the Son of God came [to the world] in the flesh [at Christmas time] by being born of a young woman of Nazareth named Mary. . . . This [was] . . . the key to God's plan to redeem the human race from sin and rebellion and restore [humankind] . . . to His friendship" (Alan Schreck, *Your Catholic Faith: A Question and Answer Catechism*, p. 28).

This December festival is adorned with a wide array of religious imagery. For example, Lutheran pastor and professor John C. McCollister has written:

> In many instances, a star is placed atop a Christmas tree as a symbol of the star that appeared at the time of Jesus's birth. The wreath represents the crown of thorns placed on the head of Jesus by the Roman soldiers just before his crucifixion. Some Christians equate Christmas gifts with the presents of gold, frankincense, and myrrh which the Wise Men brought to the Christ child. (John C. McCollister, *The Christian Book of Why*, pp. 210–212)

For Roman Catholics, even the popular Christmas carol "The Twelve Days of Christmas" has religious implications.

> The partridge in the pear tree was Jesus Christ. The two turtle doves were the Old and New Testaments. Three French hens stood for faith, hope and charity. The four calling birds were the four gospels of Matthew, Mark, Luke and John.
>
> The five golden rings recalled the Torah or Law, the first five books of the Old Testament. The six geese a-laying stood for the six days of creation. Seven swans a-swimming represented the sevenfold gifts of the Holy Spirit. The eight maids a-milking were the Eight Beatitudes.

Nine ladies dancing? These were the nine fruits of the Holy Spirit (Galatians 5). The 10 lords a-leaping were the Ten Commandments. Eleven pipers piping stood for the 11 faithful disciples. Finally, the 12 drummers symbolized the 12 points of belief in the Apostles' Creed. (St. Pius X School, Montville, NJ)

In contrast to this Jesus-centered festival of Christmas, Hanukkah is a Jewish festival rejoicing in the human victories of the dedicated few against the might of an oppressive majority. It is a reminder of the successful revolt of Mattathias and his sons, the Maccabees, in overturning the religious persecution of a Syrian Greek tyrant, Antiochus, who had tried to suppress the practice of Judaism and to impose his own pagan ritual practices. Whereas Christmas replaces the Jewish understanding of Torah with Jesus, Hanukkah insists that no person, faith, or even a king can ever replace Torah for us. Inspired by God's revelation of Torah, a small band of Maccabees defeated the mighty Syrian army, demonstrating the biblical adage, "Not by power or by might" but rather by God alone does true human success depend.

Hanukkah is the affirmation of Jewish peoplehood against the philosophy of assimilation. Dr. Ronald Brauner of Pittsburgh has observed: "[The real message of Hanukkah is that] if we are interested in the perpetuation of Judaism, then our focus, at some point, must [be the recognition that] . . . we are not like everybody else; we do hold distinctively different values and perceptions of truth . . . distinct from our non-Jewish fellow Americans" (Ronald Brauner, "Hanukah," p.2).

The Maccabees did not did seek a human embodiment of God to save them; they acted decisively on behalf of their own unique form of religious freedom. Genuinely celebrating both Hanukkah and Christmas—the primacy of God's Torah and its *mitzvot* (commandments) plus the turning away from Torah Law (Christianity's turning instead to Jesus)—is inconsistent and misleading.

PASSOVER IS NOT EASTER

For Christians, Easter commemorates the death and resurrection of Jesus. For Catholics, Jesus's death is seen as a salvation experience for humankind. Jesus is viewed as the "lamb of God" whose crucifixion offers to redeem all persons from their sins. Protestants stress the resurrection dimension of Easter. For Christianity, resurrection augurs a potential victory over death and on to eternal life.

> Easter, the festival which commemorates the resurrection of Jesus from the dead . . . [is] the center of all [Protestant] Christian theology. [Protestant] Christians believe that Jesus's resurrection provided proof that he was the Son of God and has given to all of his followers eternal life (John McCollister, *The Christian Book of Why*, p. 230)

> The bodily resurrection of Jesus Christ from the dead is a central Catholic belief, perhaps *the* central Catholic belief. . . . The resurrection of Jesus is the act of God that reveals that death, sin [the punishments for original sin], and Satan have been conquered. Therefore, Easter, the feast of Jesus's resurrection, is the most important holy day for Catholics (Alan Schreck, *Your Catholic Faith: A Question and Answer Catechism*, p. 36)

In contrast to Easter's profound religious meaning, centered around Jesus as the messiah and son of God, Passover, Judaism's most popular and powerful home ritual, is focused exclusively upon the relationship of the Jewish people with God alone. For Jews, Passover celebrates human freedom, the Exodus, and the Israelites' recommitment to the God of their ancestors. Passover is the annual reenactment of the miraculous departure of the biblical Jewish people from Egyptian bondage as a result of God's intervention. The Passover *Haggadah* does not even mention the name of the greatest Jew of all time, Moses; by comparison to God's role in the Exodus, Moses, or even the future messiah, is of limited consequence. Passover is a commemoration of *God's* miracles, *God's* hearing the cry of the oppressed, *God's* fulfillment of His promise to redeem Abraham's descendants from Egypt, *God's* ability to subvert a king (Pharaoh), an army, and an array of pagan gods.

To transmit loyalty to both Easter and Passover is only possible if one omits the religious content of both holidays and trivializes them into empty family meals, devoid of spiritual substance and sustenance.

—————— Appendix II ——————

Grandparenting Jewish Children

B ecoming a grandmother or grandfather of a Jewish child leaves Jews today with a mixture of feelings. On the one hand, there are the obvious blessings of being a grandparent:

> To become a grandparent is to become aware of the possibilities of hoping for and peering into the intangible but real future, the future that, with God's blessing, is his [my grandchild's] – beyond my death. . . .
>
> [It is that] tomorrow that I am able to project myself into. . . . My attachment to him [my grandchild] is truly in the realm of the mysterious spirit. The world of the intangible but real spirit has, for me, issued from the world of the natural order and creation. (Max Ticktin, "The Blessings of Being a Grandfather," pp. 382–383)

On the other hand, there are anxieties posed by rising rates of intermarriage and other threats to the Jewish future of one's family.

Today's grandparents of Jewish children have added responsibilities for transmitting Judaism in a caring, nurturing fashion. The prospect of Jewish continuity for your descendants may well depend upon your becoming Jewishly affirming role models. In fact, grandparents often are the best vehicles for this transmission.

> Grandparents [can] transmit religious faith and values. Grandchildren tend to see grandparents as being "closer to God" because of their age. In many of the families we visited, the

grandparents were the ones who took the children to church or temple. Although research has shown that religious behavior in children is affected most by their parents' beliefs and behavior, grandparents who take religious commitment seriously put a brake on parental indifference to questions of ultimate concern. (Arthur Kornhaber and Kenneth L. Woodward, *Grandparents and Grandchildren: The Vital Connection*, p. 170)

Professor Robert Coles of Harvard indicates in *The Spirituality of the Child*, that it is remarkable how often children refer to the ways their grandparents have influenced them. They remember the prayers, the parables, and the admonitions shared with them by another generation. At the personal level, it was from my mother's grandparents, my Bubba and my Zayda, that I learned a love for Yiddish language, European foods, and a sense of extended *mishpochah*. And it was from my mother's parents, my Nanny and my Pops, that I internalized a sense of synthesis for the equal importance of both American *and* Jewish values. In both words and deeds, grandparenting offers powerful transmission.

1. Rabbi, since I have not been "religious" up to this point, wouldn't it be hypocritical to begin to stress to my children and grandchildren that being Jewish is important to me?

It is true that by being involved in Jewish religious practices in the home and prayer at home and in the synagogue, a grandparent is provided with a natural framework to advocate Jewishness. Keep in mind that it is never too late to adopt such commitments! They will have a cumulative effect upon your extended family, building memories and shaping Judaism's relevance in your lives.

Do not be intimidated by the prospect that your son or daughter will question you: "How come you are doing these

Jewish things now, when you didn't do them when we were growing up?"

Feel empowered to answer honestly: "I have grown as a Jewish person. I now realize, more than before, just how important Jewish content is to my life. Furthermore, I want you to be aware that it is not by coincidence that our family and other families have changed in this way. One generation ago American synagogue life was dominated by decorum. Small children were not encouraged to come to services. We fell into that pattern in raising you, just as did our peers with their offspring. Today many synagogues have been reconstituted to be 'user friendly' for youngsters. Many congregations provide family services, Torah-for-tots, mini-*minyan*, and a wide range of similar programs. Also, unlike the past, the 1990s gift shops offer an incredibly wide selection of child-centered Judaica — videos, tapes, crafts, games, books."

2. How powerful are rituals in the transmission process?

Jewish ritual practices have enormous spiritual power, not only on the grandchildren but also on all other family members. Given the latent power of ritual activity, it is crucial that Jewish extended families regain ownership of Jewish ritual objects for their homes. This ownership empowers them to transmit to their grandchildren a visceral feeling of closeness to Judaism. It is the smells, sights, sounds, touch, hands-on experience of Jewishness that will last, not merely intellectual arguments. How many of us think back fondly and powerfully to childhood Passover *seders*, Hanukkah candlelighting and other candlelighting occasions, High Holy Day experiences, tasty holiday foods, special aromas associated with Jewish settings, and so on.

My own children have benefited greatly from the cumulative memories of the Jewishness of their grandparents: my mother-in-law's delicious Jewish holiday recipes, and my father-in-law's annual constructing of our *sukkah*, chopping of the fish for gefilte fish, leading the search for *hametz* prior to Passover, negotiating for the *afikoman* at the *seder*. Author Julie Hilton Danan observed:

> My fondest Jewish memories are of the Passover Sederim at my maternal grandmother's house. So many relatives were crowded into one tiny room. As we chanted the Haggadah, the heavenly aroma of the festival meal permeated the small space. My cousins and I loved to sing the holiday songs. . . . We plotted and planned our strategy for hiding the afikoman and for bargaining for our reward upon its return. (Julie Hilton Danan, *The Jewish Parents' Almanac*, p. 232)

In earlier generations, our Bubbies' and Zaydas' homes inspired us as Jews, because they contained all types of Jewish ritual objects—family Bibles, prayerbooks, *tallis*, tefillin, *yarmulkas*, candlesticks, *mezuzahs*, *hallah* board and knife, *Kiddush* cups, Passover *seder* plate, and so much else. Today, we have surrendered ownership of many of these magical tools to the synagogue. Rabbi Harold Schulweis has lamented: "Even among those Jews who are Jewishly affiliated, a growing chasm exists between the synagogue and school on the one hand, and the home on the other hand. . . . The Siddur, Machzor, Bible, prayer-shawl and skullcap are public property. Nothing is privately owned" (Harold Schulweis, "My Zeyda, His Grandchildren, and the Synagogue"). Acquire these potent ritual tools and learn how to use them meaningfully in your home, both with and without your grandchildren present. Doing this will greatly enrich your personal spiritual life and also create superb role modeling for the youngsters.

A shared Shabbat dinner speaks volumes about the beauty of Jewish life and observance. A Hanukah party, Pesach seder, Purim seudah, building a Sukkah—all of these are concrete and vivid examples of the richness of Jewish life. If we take the time to make hallah with our grandchildren, we need give them no lectures on the beauty of the Sabbath. The activity itself tells them all they need to know. The more involved the grandparent is, the greater the storehouse of memories grandchildren carry into their future lives. (Hadassah Ribalow Nadich, "The Art of Grandparenting," pp. 22–23)

Don't limit the Jewish rituals imparted to your grand-children to December and April, as competition to Christmas and Easter. Such a diminution of the riches of the Jewish ritual calendar is doomed to fail, since this twice-a-year technique places isolated Jewish holidays such as Hanukkah and Pass-over as a contrast to the public hype the media and even our general society give to Christianity's two primary celebrations. Social worker Karen Oleon Wagener cautions:

Don't try to create elaborate Hanukah festivities simply to com-pete with Christmas, advises Linda Fife (USCJ). . . . Instead, she advises that they emphasize all of the Jewish holidays throughout the year. . . .

"I call it Santa-Claus-trophobia," concurs Rabbi Harold Schul-weis. . . . "The whole world is into Christmas. But it's an artifi-cial issue—you can't pin your whole religious identity on one holiday."

Grandparents, he suggests, should help provide their grand-children with a solid Jewish base by making holiday celebrations a part of their life. "The Christmas Dilemma must start with the Rosh Hashanah Solution," he counsels. "If a kid can sleep in a sukkah, he won't want to sleep in a creche."

Year-round Jewish observance may pose a challenge for some grandparents, but, ultimately, it may be the only response to intermarriage. (Deborah Kaye, "Grandma Wrestles with Santa," p. 39)

A valuable collection of holiday activities can be found in Joel Grishaver's *40 Things You Can Do to Save the Jewish People*, as well as in his forthcoming *Activities for Jewish Grandparenting*.

3. What do I say if my children accept my newfound Jewish lifestyle for my home but refuse to encourage Jewish activities for my grandchildren within their own domain?

If that is the case, then clarify the following game plan with your son or daughter and spouse: "Although disappointed, we recognize at this point your reluctance or unwillingness to intensify the Jewish content of your home. We intend to assume a significant role in the transmitting of our Jewish heritage to our grandchildren. We will do so whenever they visit our home. We will be taking them to services with us, since that is our current practice on *Shabbat* and holidays. We will be sending them gifts of Judaica toys, games, tapes, and books that will help to make Judaism enjoyable for them. We are always ready to help you to introduce Jewish ritual and practice into your household, but we will respect and abide by whatever decisions you make concerning your household, just as we are certain that you will honor our choices inside our house."

In order to follow through on this strategy, be prepared to acknowledge gaps in your own Jewish knowledge and show a willingness to learn along with your grandchildren. Author Sunie Levin has observed:

> In your concern for imparting Jewish values to your grandchild, you will probably discover great gaps in your own knowledge. . . . [Until now] not-particularly observant Jews are often startled by the depth of feeling aroused in them when their children marry outside Judaism. They want to perpetuate a Jewish identity in their grandchildren, but they are not sure how to bring this

about—or even, for them, what a "Jewish identity" really means. (Sunie Levin, *Mingled Roots: A Guide for Jewish Grandparents of Interfaith Grandchildren*, p. 149)

The following is a checklist of many Jewish grandparenting activities. You can engage in some of these even if you live a distance away from your grandchildren:

- Subscribe to Judaic book clubs and magazines for grandchildren to help keep them abreast of Jewish issues.

- Make regular phone calls before holidays, *Shabbat*, and family occasions. Keep the relationship between parents, grandparents, and children fresh and alive.

- Write letters and cards for special occasions, especially at Jewish holiday times, enclosing special items as a basis for future communication and connection.

- Tell bedtime stories tied to holidays, to *Shabbat*, and to Jewish memories of the family.

- Conduct Judaica memory trips, even for an afternoon, to the "old neighborhood," as well as visits to Jewish museums (especially children-oriented hands-on exhibits).

- Create a memory drawer or trunk for items you have used on Jewish holidays or other observances, or establish "time capsules" from your past (to be opened on special occasions).

- Collect a Jewish library so that children can learn from and be influenced by the presence of Judaica books. A subset of the home library should be resources for youngsters, such as *One-Minute Bible Stories* by Shari Lewis, *The Jewish Kids Catalog* by Chaya Burstein, *A Kid's Catalogue of Israel* by Chaya Burstein, and *God's Paintbrush* by Sandy Eisenberg Sasso.

- Help your grandchild collect audio- and videotapes and CDs with *Shabbat* and holiday songs, as well as games, stories, plays, activities, and coloring books with similar themes.

- Do not underestimate the potential laden in visits with your grandchildren.

Your visit is a golden opportunity to build strong family bonds. Grandparent visits with shared experiences can bind the extended family members together. As your grandchild grows older, the rituals of family visits become part of their heritage. Like great-grand-mother's old family recipe, a fondness for certain customs is often passed down through the generations. As a grandchild becomes an adult, singing special songs and enjoying family jokes will become cherished and wonderful memories. (Sunie Levin, "When You Visit Your Grandchildren," p. 20)

4. How shall we pursue the goal of making our grandchild into a good Jew, a *mensch*?"

Judaism has a great deal of wisdom and guidance for every aspect of our life. It is not confined to the walls of the synagogue. It can help reinforce ethical values that parents seek to impart to the newest generation. One interviewee reflected to researcher Martha Fay, regarding the benefit to sending a child to Sunday school: "It is not so much what they are learning as that they hear it *there*. We talk about all the same things at home, but just as when we talk about school things at home, they don't take it as seriously as they do in school. There is an added seriousness to these issues because they heard about it elsewhere as well" (Martha Fay, *Do Children Need Religion? How Parents Today Are Thinking About the Big Questions*, p. 83).

By linking right and wrong to a "Higher Authority," grandparents impart a sense of conscience to our youngsters. Here is an example of how *tzedakah* via a grandparent became part of the home life of Shimon Paskow:

To my Bubbe, righteousness meant charity, and Bubbe was a very charitable woman. She had pushkes, charity boxes, in the kitchen and her bedroom. There were round charity boxes, square ones and rectangular ones. . . .

The pushkes came not only in different shapes, sizes and colors, but also with attractive pictures and inscriptions. Some had sketches of stone buildings with domes, others with impressive pictures of eminent rabbis with long beards and different hats. One wore a very large yarmulka; another, a big black hat with a wide brim; and one even had a fur hat, called a streimel. . . .

The monies collected in the pushkes went to yeshivas, orphanages, soup kitchens, the poor, revered rabbis, homes for the aged, sanitariums, Eretz Yisrael, etc. . . . I, too, sometimes deposited a few pennies into the slots. . . .

Physically, Bubbe is gone, but her memory lives on in me. . . .

(Shimon Paskow, "I Remember Bubbe: The Receipts of Righteousness," p. 3)

5. Should I offer to finance the Jewish experiences of my grandchildren?

Many grandparents put away zero coupon bonds for college as an investment in the grandchild's professional future. Similarly, they need to do what they can to ensure the youngster's Jewish future. At birth, why not begin to put away dollars to help fund the necessary but expensive ingredients for imparting Jewishness to children:

- Synagogue affiliation

- Jewish education

- Jewish informal activities: Jewish camping, youth groups, Israel travel, etc.

- Jewish networking at college and beyond

SYNAGOGUE AFFILIATION

The formation of a Jewish youngster's religious identity benefits immeasurably by the family's affiliation with a specific
congregation, enabling the children to identify with a particular rabbi, cantor, religious educator, and the like. Make sure
that you are affiliated with a congregation, and urge your
daughter or son and family to join their local synagogue as
early as possible in your grandchild's life.

This is a very important step. It defines an American family
as being serious or lacking seriousness about their religion. If
financial considerations are a barrier to their affiliation, it
would be wise to provide monetary assistance if you can, or to
contact the local rabbi for guidance.

Religious moments build a sense of comfort for the grandchildren as they encounter sacred spaces in synagogues and as
they interact with the Torah and with religious leaders.

JEWISH EDUCATION

With regard to formal Jewish studies, do not let your son or
daughter fall into the trap of asking the child whether her or
she wants to attend. We know that formal Jewish education is
critically important for our youngsters. Do not have them vote
upon their desire to attend, anymore than they are permitted
to make choices about secular education.

JEWISH INFORMAL ACTITITIES

Similarly, do not permit your son or daughter to leave to a
child's whims the critical decisions regarding Jewish informal
experiences. Jewish communal and peer group activities offer
memories that accrue in day camp, overnight camp, youth
groups, a teen group experience in Israel, *tzedakah* projects,
JCC activities, and more. The opportunity for youngsters who

are raised as a minority in a non-Jewish society to feel the warmth and comfort, the self-esteem and pride, of being part of collective Jewish endeavors of their peers—cannot be over-estimated. The "informal education" transmitted in this fashion should become an indispensable part of your Jewish family life agenda. As with synagogue affiliation or religious school, do not allow finances to be a barrier to your grandchild's participation. If necessary, provide subsidies for these critically important investments in your family's Jewish future. You will never regret the dollars spent!

COLLLEGE AND BEYOND

The formation of a Jewish identity does not conclude with twelfth grade. If possible, offer to contribute to the financing of a grandchild's college if a suitable environment is selected. Grandparents should advocate that their grandchildren explore college options that include viable Jewish student populations, a Hillel Foundation, and nearby synagogue communities. Only college populations with substantial percentages of Jewish students will provide adequate peer group experiences. The B'nai B'rith Hillel Foundation evaluated Jewish student life on almost every campus your high schooler might consider. Consult their guide when the college search begins, usually during the junior year of high school.

And after graduation do whatever is possible to link single grandchildren to singles programs, networks, dating services, adult education, community service projects, and social justice activism offered under Jewish sponsorship. Most young people will select a marital partner not on the basis of ideology but rather because of propinquity, that is, they will marry the people they meet. Increasing opportunities are arising for single Jewish young adults to meet one another in non-threatening settings.

CONCLUSION

Grandparents should not leave the Jewish future of their grandchildren to chance. Instead, we must develop a strategy to give our grandsons and granddaughters meaningful encounters with Judaism's joys, spiritual fulfillment, communal enhancement, intellectual stimulation, cultural aesthetics, social action imperatives, and institutional settings.

In addition to the numerous recommendations already provided in this discussion, consider some of the following. These and other Judaica enhancements should be implemented with the intent of establishing a Jewish "rhythm," of attaining a "critical mass" of Jewish living for our young.

Given current threats to Jewish continuity, to the Jewish future of your family: You ought to make new Jewish demands on yourself and on your grandchildren.

- You must be committed to be a Jewish role model in word and deed for your grandchildren.

- You must seek out and affiliate with a suitable synagogue and religious school.

- You must engage in hands-on Jewish activities with your grandsons and granddaughters.

- You must articulate Jewish values for being a *mensch*, and must identify suitable Jewish role models and heroes.

- You must cultivate *heart* (spiritual), *head* (intellectual), and *hand* (social action) aspects of Judaism, making clear that being Jewish is very important to you.

All of the above require some effort and some determination—but they will enhance your life and that of your household, and they will transmit substantive Judaism to future generations.

Appendix III

Resource Guide

PUBLICATIONS

The following materials produced by Conservative Judaism's institutions may be ordered through the United Synagogue Book Service.

Am Kadosh: Celebrating Our Uniqueness, by Daniel H. Gordis. New York: Department of Youth Activities, United Synagogue of Conservative Judaism, 1992.

The Art of Jewish Living: Hanukkah, by Ron Wolfson. New York: Federation of Jewish Men's Clubs, 1990, especially pp. 152–191.

Checkmate/Leader's Guide to Video: "What Paul Told Sally." New York: United Synagogue of America and Union of American Hebrew Congregations, 1979, 88 pages.

Dual Faith Parenting: Second Thoughts about a Popular Trend, by Alan Silverstein. New York: Federation of Jewish Men's Clubs, 1993.

Future Thinking: The Effects of Intermarriage? by Greta Brown. New York: Commission on Jewish Education, United Synagogue of Conservative Judaism, 1993. A 10-lesson module for use with pre- and post-*bar/bat mitzvah* students with teacher's guide and student notebook.

"How To Prevent Intermarriage," by Israel Moshowitz. United Synagogue of America *Proceedings* 60 (1971): 177–184.

In God's Image: Making Jewish Decisions about the Body, by Bernard Novick. New York: Department of Youth Activities, United Synagogue of America, 1985.

Interdating: A Jewish Parent's Guide, by Alan Silverstein. New York: Women's League for Conservative Judaism, 1994.

Interdating-Intermarriage: Intervention, by Edward Edelstein. New York: Program Department, United Synagogue of Conservative Judaism, 1992. A program guide to be used in conjunction with *Intermarriage: Our Grounds for Concern.*

Intermarriage, by Ira Eisenstein. New York: United Synagogue of America, 1964.

"Intermarriage and Conservative Judaism: Communal Policy and Program Direction," by Steven Bayme. Rabbinical Assembly *Proceedings* 53 (1991): 36–46.

Intermarriage: Our Grounds for Concern—14 Questions, 14 Answers, by Alan Silverstein. New York: Commission on Jewish Education, United Synagogue of Conservative Judaism, 1992.

Intermarriage: What Can We Do? What Should We Do? New York: Program Department, United Synagogue of Conservative Judaism, 1992.

It All Begins with a Date: Parent/Young Adult Dialogues about Interdating, by Alan Silverstein. New York: United Synagogue of Conservative Judaism, 1994.

The Jewish Family Relationship, by David M. Feldman. New York: Department of Youth Activities, United Synagogue of America, 1975.

"Jewish Love, Jewish Law: Can Liberal Judaism Weather the Intermarriage Crisis?" by Daniel H. Gordis. *Jewish Spectator* 56:3 (Winter 1991/1992): 6–11.

Love and Sex: A Modern Jewish Perspective, by Robert Gordis. New York: Women's League for Conservative Judaism, 1978.

"The Mitzvah of Endogamy: Marriage Within the Faith," by Jerome Epstein. New York: United Synagogue of Conservative Judaism, 1992.

Parent Education for Parents of Adolescents, (teachers' manual). New York: Commission on Jewish Education, United Synagogue of America, 1986.

"Perils and Prevention of Intermarriage," by Saul I. Teplitz. United Synagogue of America *Proceedings* 52 (1965): 70–76.

Prevention of Intermarriage, Jewish Family Living Series. New York: Women's League for Conservative Judaism, 1972–1973.

Promoting Jewish Continuity for Children Ages 3–6: A Guide for Early Childhood Educators, Rabbis, Lay Leaders and Concerned Parents, by Alan Silverstein. Caldwell, NJ: CAI Publishing, 1995.

A Return to the Mitzvah of Endogamy, by Jerome Epstein. New York: United Synagogue of Conservative Judaism, 1992.

We Are Family, by Joel S. Wasser. New York: Department of Youth Activities, United Synagogue of America, 1991.

Why Be Jewish Now? edited by Ron and Leora Isaacs. Department of Youth Activities. Kadima Encampment, Hillside, NJ, Hagalil Region, Source Book and Leader's Guide, 1988.

"Why Be Jewish? What's the Gain, the Pride, the Joy?" (pamphlet), by Alan Silverstein. New York: United Synagogue of Conservative Judaism, 1994. Teachers' and students' guide has been prepared by Susan Werk and Shelley Kniaz for use with pre-*bar/bat mitzvah* families as well as with teens.

Your Child: For Parents of Young Jewish Children. New York: Commission on Jewish Education, United Synagogue of Conservative Judaism. Subscriptions are available for this journal, which is published three times a year.

ADDITIONAL RECOMMENDED READING

"American Jewry: Which Way?" symposium in *Hadassah Magazine* 74:10 (June/July 1993): 10–50.

"Are Jews' Objections to Intermarriage Racist?" by Dennis Prager. *Ultimate Issues* 9:2 (April–June 1993): 13–16.

"But Mom, We're Just Dating!" by Elliot Fein. New York: Conference on the Advancement of Jewish Education (CAJE). Lessons and sourcebook. *Bikkurim* 9:3 (Summer 1992): 26–27.

"Children of the Intermarried" (pamphlet), by Egon Mayer. New York: American Jewish Committee, 1983.

"The Dilemma of Intermarriage," in Max Routtenberg, *Seedtime and Harvest.* New York: Bloch, 1969, pp. 135–161.

Ethnic Identity and Marital Conflict, by Joel Crohn. New York: American Jewish Committee, 1985.

Hawking God: A Young Jewish Woman's Ordeal in Jews for Jesus, by Ellen Kamentsky. Medford, MA: Sapphire Press, 1992.

Highlights of the CJF 1990 National Jewish Population Survey. New York: Council of Jewish Federations, 1991.

How to Stop an Intermarriage, by Kalman Packouz. New York: Feldheim, 1984.

"The Hyphen Between the Cross and the Star," in Harold Schulweis, ed., *God's Mirror.* New York: KTAV, 1990.

Image of the Jewish Woman: Myth and Reality. Washington, DC: B'nai B'rith Women, 1640 Rhode Island Avenue, N.W., 1986. Audiotape as well as educational materials.

Intermarriage, by Albert Gordon. Boston: Beacon Press, 1964.

"Intermarriage and the Jewish Future" (pamphlet), by Egon Mayer and Carl Shengold. New York: American Jewish Committee, 1979.

The Intermarriage Crisis, edited by Steven Bayme. New York: American Jewish Committee, 1993.

The Intermarriage Crisis: Jewish Communal Perspectives and Responses. New York: American Jewish Committee, 1991.

Jewish Alternatives in Love, Dating and Marriage, by Pinchas Stolper. New York: National Conference of Synagogue Youth, 1984.

Jewish Identity and Self-Esteem: Healing Wounds Through Ethnotherapy, by Judith Weinstein Klein. New York: American Jewish Committee, 1989.

Jews for Nothing: On Cults, Intermarriage and Assimilation by Dov Aharoni Fisch. New York: Feldheim, 1984.

The Jewish Way in Love and Marriage, by Maurice Lamm. New York: Harper & Row, 1980, especially pp. 48–65 discussing interfaith marriage.

"Mixed Marriage," chapter 14 in Roland Gittelsohn, *The Extra Dimension: A Jewish View of Marriage.* New York: Union of American Hebrew Congregations, 1982.

The Nine Questions People Ask about Judaism, by Dennis Prager and Joseph Telushkin. New York: Simon & Schuster, 1981. See the chapter "Why Shouldn't I Intermarry?"

On Being A Jew, by James Kugel. San Francisco: HarperCollins, 1990.

"The Prohibition Against Intermarriage," chapter 13 in David Bleich, *Contemporary Halachic Problems*, vol. 2. New York: KTAV, 1983.

Psychology and Jewish Identity Education, by Perry London and Barry Chazan. New York: American Jewish Committee, 1990.

Questions Jewish Parents Ask about Intermarriage, by Mark L. Winer and Aryeh Meir. New York: American Jewish Committee, 1992.

"Thirteen Principles of Intermarriage," by Dennis Prager. *Ultimate Issues* 8:4 (October–December 1992): 6–7.

Where Judaism Differed, by Abba Hillel Silver. Philadelphia: Jewish Publication Society, 1977.

Who Needs God? by Harold Kushner. New York: Simon & Schuster (Summit Books), 1989.

"Why Be Jewish?" (pamphlet), by Barry Holtz and Steven Bayme. New York: American Jewish Committee, 1994.

"Why Be Jewish," symposium. *Moment* 17:6 (December 1992): 36–51.

"Why I Am a Jew: The Case for a Religious Life," by Dennis Prager. *Ultimate Issues* 2:2–3 (Spring–Summer 1987): 27.

VIDEOTAPES AND FILMS

"Ethnotherapy with Jews." 42 minutes. A videocassette and discussion guide, based on group-encounter dialogues and research findings on positive and negative feelings toward Judaism and Jewishness. American Jewish Committee, New York.

"The Great Difference." 13 minutes. Trigger film focusing on interfaith couples and the decisions they face. Direct Cinema Ltd., P.O. Box 69799, Los Angeles, CA 90069.

"Intermarriage: When Love Meets Tradition." 28 minutes plus 36-page discussion guide. Focusing on five interfaith couples in a candid portrait of the problems they face. Cinema Limited, P.O. Box 69799, Los Angeles, CA 90069.

"Lisa's Dilemma." 6 minutes. A trigger film to promote discussion about the effects of intermarriage on the children of such unions. Toronto Jewish Congress, 150 Beverly Street, Toronto, Ontario M5T 1Y6, Canada.

"The Myth of the Melting Pot Marriage: Ethnotherapy with Jewish–Gentile Couples." 30 minutes. Maps the terrain of interpersonal and identity issues in Jewish/non-Jewish marriages, indicating the consequences of intermarriage. American Jewish Committee, New York.

"What Paul Told Sally." 12-minute trigger film in which Jewish teens discuss the issues of interdating. United Synagogue of Conservative Judaism, New York.

"Where Judaism Differed." Five hour-long videocassettes exploring Judaism's relationship to paganism, Hellenism, Christianity, Islam, and modernity. American Jewish Committee, New York.

"Why Does Love Fail So Often?" Interviews by Rabbi Allen Maller with Jewish divorced persons whose interfaith marriages failed due to religious/cultural strains. A lesson plan is available for discussion by youth and adults. Rabbi Allen Maller, Akiba Video, Culver City, CA.

Promoting Jewish Continuity: Opportunities Available within Conservative Judaism

EARLY CHILDHOOD

Enrollment in early childhood programs under Jewish institutional auspices has skyrocketed to record highs. For more than a decade, preschool has represented the major growth area in the spectrum of Jewish schooling experience.

Two hundred and fifty of our Conservative congregations currently have nursery school two to five days a week for children 2 to 5 years old. Many more run Sunday morning or one-day-a-week programs for children 5 to 7 years old as part of the synagogue school. The increasing demand by parents for quality nursery school education in our Conservative congregations provides a challenging educational opportunity. Nursery schools serve as an essential gateway for early Jewish education for both children and parents, encourage synagogue membership, and help expand communal involvement.

SYNAGOGUE SCHOOLS

In 1987–1988, the last years for which we have data, 43 percent of supplementary schools were under Conservative sponsorship. This constituted some 800 schools with about 108,000 students, according to the report of the Division on Jewish Demography of the Institute of Contemporary Jewry at the Hebrew University of Jerusalem.

There are effective, exciting synagogue schools in North America that produce knowledgeable, committed, and caring

Jewish adults. Some of the characteristics of a quality school are:

- A "holistic" approach to learning, where there is an integration of the school program with all aspects of Jewish life—inside and outside of synagogue. The synagogue school experience begins in nursery school and extends into adulthood. It is multidimensional and extends to youth groups (Kadima and United Synagogue Youth [USY]), camp experiences (Ramah and USY on Wheels), and Israel trips (Ramah and USY). The professionals and lay leadership of all these areas work together so that education extends beyond the four walls of the classroom.

- A vision that informs the style and direction of the curriculum, methodologies, and feel of the school. This vision matches both the ideology of the Conservative movement and the goals of the community.

- A constant desire to improve that entails attending to problems and challenges, frequent self-evaluation, discussion, and a willingness to try new things.

- The retention of students through the high-school years.

- A high level of participation in rich and frequent family programs.

- Careful attention to the environment—how the physical setting, rules, policies, and personal interactions teach our students.

- Experiences that both form and transform, that create a lasting effect on individuals.

- A significant professional development program.

- An understanding that the education of the next generation is a raison d'être of the synagogue.

SOLOMON SCHECHTER DAY SCHOOLS

Founded in 1956–1957 and nurtured by the United Synagogue of Conservative Judaism, the Solomon Schechter Day School movement has grown to 65 schools with more than 16,000 students and employing more than 2,000 educators in general and Jewish studies. There has been consistent growth in the Schechter schools over the last few years, in spite of a period of economic recession, and they have achieved great credibility throughout America. The schools attract a broad segment of the Jewish population, and students think of the dual program as a natural environment.

CAMPS RAMAH

Ramah is a system of six regional overnight camps, a day camp, and year-round Israel programs. We service, at present, 4,500 youths each summer, 1,200 college-age staff, 500 units in our family camps, and another 2,000 children in synagogue and day-school weekends.

It is the experience of intensive immersion in a total environment of Jewish learning practices, arts, sports, and the tasks of daily living that lead toward personal commitment. One becomes a "Ramah-nik" forever. Over the years, involvement with Ramah has led to a committed population of Jews who, more often than not, affiliate with and support the Conservative movement.

The Camp Ramah experience is clearly a denominational one, and it is among the most powerful tools for imparting Jewish values, identity, and practical knowledge consistent with the Conservative movement. It is crucial to create a level field of opportunity for people to attend Ramah so that denominational camping can compete with other camping opportunities and enrich congregational life.

YOUTH MOVEMENTS

Youth programs under the sponsorship of the United Synagogue of Conservative Judaism include close to 25,000 members of Kadima and USY in more than 750 local affiliates throughout North America.

USY, founded in 1951, is for high-school-age participants, while Kadima, founded in 1968, is for those in grades 6 through 8. Affiliated chapters are divided into 17 regions, each with a director and well-established infrastructure.

Our synagogue youth movement is an integral component in the Jewish educational process and should be regarded as more than a social outlet. It provides our youth with an opportunity for a serious exploration of Jewish identity and nurtures their involvement in adult Jewish life.

Most Kadima programs focus on the local chapter, with some regional programs held on an occasional basis. Kadima publishes its own quarterly magazine, which is distributed to all members. Programming and educational materials for advisers are produced on a regular basis.

USY offers programs on the local, regional, and national levels. Locally there is a broad variety of balanced programming including religious, educational, and recreational components. Most regional and national programs focus on the educational and religious components. Regions sponsor several weekend *kinnusim* (retreats), some of which are home-hospitality weekends, while others are held at hotels or campsites. Most regions sponsor a weeklong camp program at the conclusion of the regular camping season. All weekend and encampment programs include an educational component based around a central theme. Regions also run training programs for advisers and often issue their own publications and materials.

The national office sponsors an annual convention over the winter recess, held in a different city each year. Depending upon locations, the convention attracts between 1,000 and 1,200 participants each year. A new theme is studied annually and an educational text exploring the annual theme through classical Jewish texts and experiential activities is produced.

USY sponsors the USY Israel Pilgrimage, a six-week summer Israel program that attracts about 600 participants. It also sponsors USY on Wheels, the only cross-country bus tour for high-school students that is kosher and *shomer Shabbat*. Both programs include an organized educational structure. USY also sponsors the Nativ Year program in Israel for entering college freshmen, with the Hebrew University, and USY High, an eight-week academic program for high-school students in cooperation with the Alexander Muss High School in Israel.

In addition, USY produces a broad array of educational materials for its members and staff.

The synagogue youth movement must be seen as a critical ingredient in fostering Jewish continuity. Kadima and USY can provide the opportunity for a serious exploration of one's identity in a nonthreatening environment.

ISRAEL EXPERIENCE

The Conservative movement sponsors 12 different Israel experience programs through Ramah and USY. Given the statistics that indicate the positive impact of an Israel experience in shaping a young person's Jewish identity, there must be a more concerted effort to attract greater numbers while continuing to increase the quality of the programs. At the present time, more than 1,000 people visit Israel through Ramah and USY.

The advantage of Israel programs affiliated with synagogue movements is that each participant returns home to a specific context and has the opportunity to process the experience with a circle of young people and adults who share a common frame of reference. This ensures that the Israel experience is part of a continuum, not an isolated experience.

COLLEGE LIFE

Hillel is the "Jewish address" on campus, and the Conservative Jewish presence is KOACH. We cooperate with Hillel on a variety of levels: KOACH professionals participate in Hillel student leadership conferences, attend the Hillel professional conference, and develop contacts with Hillel directors across the continent.

We are able to enhance the Hillel program in a number of different ways. The KOACH Creative Grants Program awards campuses up to $2,000 a year to develop programming for Conservative Jewish students. Activities have varied, from *Shabbatonim* to social action projects, to *kosher l'Pesah* kitchens to egalitarian *minyanim*, to social activities to academic presentations.

Our KOACH publications have increased in quality and quantity. A newsletter is published three times a year (distributed via direct mail and through Hillel Foundations), and special pamphlets are issued on different topics. These include Rabbi Neil Gillman's *Guide for the New Jewish College Student*, which is distributed to all college freshmen who were registered members of USY.

An annual KOACH *kallah* is held every February, bringing together students from campuses throughout North America. Regional weekends are also held in various parts of the country, enabling students to network with other like-minded young people who are interested in creating a vibrant Conservative community during their college years and beyond.

Coordination of efforts with our Center on Campus in Jerusalem has increased our activity in Israel for students spending time abroad. Assistance to congregations who serve college-age populations (both home and away) have also increased.

For general information, see *The Hillel Guide to Jewish Life on Campus*, available from the Hillel Foundation, 1640 Rhode Island Avenue N.W., Washington, DC 20036.

ADULT EDUCATION

Conservative Judaism has the resources to meet the challenges posed by adult education. We have a long history of translating Judaism into a modern idiom. Indeed, adult education represents a critical vehicle for intensifying Jewish continuity.

- It can provide meaningful adult role-modeling for children enrolled in formal Jewish education.

- It can upgrade the quality of Jewish institutional leadership.

- It can stimulate non-Jewish relatives of Jews to contemplate sincere conversion to Judaism.

- It can temper the alienation of many Jewish students during their campus years.

In the words of Rabbi William Lebeau, dean of the rabbinical school of the Jewish Theological Seminary, we need adult education: "[as a mode of action] when a Jew cries out for God, community or spiritual guidance. . . . To inspire . . . [uninvolved] Jews to commit to serious Jewish study and observance. . . . To find ways to challenge [knowledgeable Jews] to climb higher on the ladder of learning and commitment" (William H. Lebeau, "To Learn, to Teach, and to Observe: The Critical Role of Adult Education for Our Future," pp. 14–15).

Effective adult Jewish education has frequently been identified with large lecture hall and scholar-in-residence settings in which single-occasion gatherings of a passive nature can involve hundreds of Jewish men and women.

Given today's complex social climate, we need diverse formats and locations serving a growing variety of needs, lifestyles, ages, and interest groups. The following represent examples of this necessary diversity of adult learning venues:

- Hebrew literacy courses
- Holiday workshops—Passover, Hanukkah, etc.
- Introduction to Judaism and Jewish literacy courses
- Adult *bar/bat mitzvah*
- Parent education and family education programs
- Synagogue study *havurot*
- Community-wide public lectures
- Study groups at law firms, health care centers, financial institutions, etc.
- Senior citizens' "life-long learning" courses
- Talmud study circles
- Congregational adult education courses
- Radio interviews
- Audiocassette tapes of lectures and classes
- Retreats at Camps Ramah and other locations
- Learners' *minyan* programs at synagogues

The Conservative movement—our local synagogues, our United Synagogue Regional Programs, our educational outreach efforts by the Jewish Theological Seminary—has the materials as well as available personnel to meet these challenges.

Bibliography

Abramowitz, Yosef. "Why be Jewish?" *Moment* 17:6 (December 1992): 45–48.

Anker, Charlotte. "We Are the Children You Warned Our Parents About." *Moment* 16:1 (February 1991): 34–39.

Attarian, John. Book review of Michael Medved's *Hollywood vs. America*. *Crisis* 11:9 (1993): 55.

Bellah, Robert, et al. *Habits of the Heart*. New York: Harper & Row, 1985.

Berger, Peter. *The Heretical Imperative*. New York: Bantam Books, 1989.

Bleich, David. "The Prohibition Against Intermarriage." In David Bleich, ed., *Contemporary Halachic Problems*, vol 2. New York: KTAV, 1983.

Bloom, Harold. *The American Religion*. New York: Simon & Schuster, 1992.

B'nai B'rith Women. "The Image of the Jewish Woman: Myth and Reality." Washington, DC, 1991, audiotape plus packet of educational materials.

Brauner, Ronald. "Hanukah." *Straightalk* 1:5 (December 1992): 2.

Coles, Robert. *The Spirituality of the Child*. Boston: Houghton Mifflin, 1990.

Cowan, Paul. *An Orphan in History*. Garden City, NY: Doubleday, 1982.

Cowan, Paul, and Cowan, Rachel. *Mixed Blessings: Marriage Between Jews and Christians*. New York: Doubleday, 1987.

Danan, Julie Hilton. *The Jewish Parents' Almanac*. Northvale, NJ: Jason Aronson, 1994.

Dershowitz, Alan. *Chutzpah*. New York: Simon & Schuster, 1992.

Donin, Hayim Halevy. *To Raise a Jewish Child*. New York: Basic Books, 1977.

Eisen, Arnold. "Abraham Joshua Heschel." New York: Jewish Theological Seminary, Fall 1992, audiotape.

——. "The Role of a Jewish Research Institute." *The Wilstein Institute Newsletter*, Spring 1993, p. 1.

Episcopal Church of America. *Book of Common Prayer*. New York: Episcopal Church of America, 1989.

Family Education Committee. *Parent Education for Parents of Adolescents*. New York: United Synagogue of America, 1976.

Fay, Martha. *Do Children Need Religion?* New York: Pantheon Books, 1993.

Fields, Harvey J. *A Torah Commentary for Our Times—Volume One: Genesis*. New York: Union of American Hebrew Congregations, 1990.

Fisch, Dov Aharoni. *Jews for Nothing*. New York: Feldheim, 1984.

Fishman, Sylvia Barack, and Goldstein, Alice. *When They Are Grown They Will Not Depart: Jewish Education and the Jewish Behavior of American Adults*. Waltham, MA: Brandeis University, 1994.

Fitzpatrick, Jean Grasso. *Something More: Nurturing Your Child's Spiritual Growth*. New York: Viking Penguin, 1991.

Fuchs, Stephen. "Reach Out—But Also Bring In." *Sh'ma* 21:12 (March 8, 1991): 10.

Gittelsohn, Roland B. *Love in Your life: A Jewish View of Teenage Sexuality*. New York: Union of American Hebrew Congregations, 1991.

Goldman, Ari. *The Search for God at Harvard*. New York: Ballantine Books, 1991.

Goodman-Malamuth, Leslie, and Margolis, Robin. *Between Two Worlds*. New York: Pocket Books, 1992.

Gordis, Daniel. *Am Kadosh: Celebrating Our Uniqueness*. New York: United Synagogue Youth, 1993.

Gordis, Robert et al. *Emet Ve-Emunah: Statement of Principles of Conservative Judaism*. New York: Rabbinical Assembly, Jewish Theological Seminary, United Synagogue of Conservative Judaism, 1988.

Gordon, Albert I. *Intermarriage*. Boston: Beacon Press, 1964.

Gore, Albert, Jr. *Earth in the Balance: Ecology and the Human Spirit*. Boston: Houghton Mifflin, 1992.

Greenberg, Sidney, ed. *A Modern Treasury of Jewish Thoughts*. New York: Thomas Yoseloff, 1960.

Greenberg, Simon. *A Jewish Philosophy and Pattern of Life*. New York: Jewish Theological Seminary, 1981.

Grishaver, Joel. "December Dilemma." *Jewish Family* 1:1 (December 1992): 3.

Hertzberg, Arthur. *Being Jewish in America*. New York: Schocken Books, 1978.

Heschel, Abraham Joshua. *The Sabbath*. New York: Harper Torchbooks, 1966.

"Intermarriage: When Love Meets Tradition." New York: Union of American Hebrew Congregations, 1990, videotape.

Israel, Richard. "Interdating." In Sharon Strassfeld and Kathy Green, eds., *The Jewish Family Book*. New York: Bantam Books, 1981, pp. 349–355.

Johnson, Catherine. *Lucky in Love: The Secrets of Happy Couples and How Their Marriages Thrive*. New York: Viking, 1992.

Kaplan, Mordecai. *The Future of the American Jew*. New York: MacMillan, 1948.

Kaye, Deborah. "Grandma Wrestles with Santa." *The Jewish Monthly* 108:3 (December 1993): 36–40.

Kennedy, Ruby Jo Reeves. "Single or Triple Melting Pot? Intermarriage Trends in New Haven, 1870–1940." *American Journal of Sociology* 49 (January 1944): 331–339.

Koch, Edward I. *Citizen Koch*. New York: St. Martins Press, 1992.

Kornhaber, Arthur, and Woodward, Kenneth L. *Grandparents and Grandchildren: The Vital Connection*. New Brunswick, NJ: Transaction, 1991.

Kosmin, Barry A., et al. *Highlights of the CJF 1990 National Jewish Population Survey*. New York: Council of Jewish Federations, 1991.

Kroloff, Charles. "Love and Marriage." *Keeping Posted* 19:5 (February 1974): 3–7.

Kushner, Harold. *When All You've Ever Wanted Isn't Enough*. New York: Summit Books, 1986.

———. *Who Needs God?* New York: Summit Books, 1989.

Kushner, Lawrence. *God was in this PLACE and I, i did not know*. Woodmont, VT: Jewish Lights, 1993.

Lamdan, Elimelech. "Judaism and Transcendental Meditation." In Simcha Cohen et al., eds., *Return to the Source*. New York: Feldheim, 1984, pp. 209–217.

Lamm, Maurice. *The Jewish Way in Love and Marriage.* New York: Harper & Row, 1980.

Lebeau, William H. "To Learn, to Teach, and to Observe: The Critical Role of Adult Education for Our Jewish Future." *Women's League Outlook* 62:4 (Summer 1992): 14–15.

Levey, Larry. "Why I Embraced, Then Rejected Messianic Judaism." *The Jewish Monthly* 99:7 (April 1984): 18–21.

Levin, Sunie. "When You Visit Your Grandchildren." *Kansas City Star,* April 28, 1993, p. 20.

Lipstadt, Deborah. "The Ties That No Longer Bind." *Jewish Spectator* 56:2 (Fall 1991): 62–63.

Marder, Janet. "New Perspectives on Reform Jewish Outreach." In Steven Bayme, ed., *Approaches to Intermarriage: Areas of Consensus.* New York: American Jewish Committee, 1993, pp. 5–8.

Mayer, Egon. *Children of the Intermarried.* New York: American Jewish Committee, 1983.

McCollister, John C. *The Christian Book of Why.* Middle Village, NY: Jonathan David, 1983.

Medved, Michael. *Hollywood vs. America: Popular Culture and the War on Traditional Values.* New York: HarperCollins, 1982.

Moline, Jack. "Ten Things We Do Not Say Often Enough to Our Children." Kiamesha, NY: United Synagogue Convention, 1991, audiotape.

Moline, Richard. "Choosing a College from a Jewish Perspective." *Women's League Outlook* 64:1 (February 1993): 21–22.

Nadich, Hadassah Ribalow. "The Art of Grandparenting." *Women's League Outlook* 65:4 (Summer 1994): 22–24.

Ochs, Vanessa. *Words on Fire: One Woman's Journey into the Sacred.* New York: Harcourt Brace, 1992.

Osbourne, Ronald. "Marriage of Christians and Jews." *Plumbline* 13:3 (September 1985): 9–11.

Parent Education for Parents of Adolescents. New York: Commission on Jewish Education, United Synagogue of America, 1986.

Paskow, Shimon. "I Remember Bubbe: The Receipts of Righteousness." *Jewish News* (Metrowest, New Jersey) 47:51 (December 23, 1993), p. 3.

Pearl, Jonathan, and Pearl, Judith. "The Changing Channels of TV's Intermarriage Depictions." *Jewish Televimage Report* 1:1 (June 1991): 1.

Perel, Esther, and Cowan, Rachel. "A More Perfect Union: Intermarriage and the Jewish World." *Tikkun* 7:3 (May/June 1992): 59–64.

Petsonk, Judy, and Remsen, Jim. *The Intermarriage Handbook*. New York: William Morrow & Co., 1988.

Pogrebin, Letty Cottin. *Deborah, Golda, and Me*. New York: Crown, 1991.

Prager, Dennis. "Are Jews' Objections to Intermarriage Racist?" *Ultimate Issues* 9:2 (April–June 1993): 13–16.

———. "Happiness Isn't Fun." *Ultimate Issues* 5:1 (January–March 1989): 13, 16.

———. "Is There Such a Thing as 'Jews for Jesus'?" *Ultimate Issues* 5:4 (October–December 1989): 6–7.

———. "Raising a Jewish Child in a Christian Society." Los Angeles, 1993, audiotape.

———. "Thirteen Principles of Intermarriage." *Ultimate Issues* 8:4 (October–December 1992): 6–7.

———. "Why I Am a Jew: The Case for a Religious Life." *Ultimate Issues* 2:2–3 (Spring/Summer 1986): 1–35.

Prager, Dennis, and Telushkin, Joseph. *Nine Questions People Ask About Judaism*. New York: Simon & Schuster, 1981.

Reisman, Bernard. "Informal Jewish Education in North America." A report submitted to the Commission on Jewish Education in North America. New York, 1990.

Reuben, Steven Carr. *Raising Jewish Children in a Contemporary World*. Rochlin, CA: Prima Publishing, 1992.

Romanoff, Lena. *Your People, My People*. Philadelphia: Jewish Publication Society, 1990.

Roiphe, Anne. *Generation Without Memory*. Boston: Beacon Press, 1982.

Romano, Dugan. *Intercultural Marriages: Promises and Pitfalls*. Yarmouth, ME: Intercultural Press, 1988.

Roth, Philip. *The Counterlife*. New York: Farrar, Straus, Giroux, 1986.

Routtenberg, Max. *Seedtime and Harvest*. New York: Bloch, 1969.

Rudin, Jacob Philip. *A Harvest of Forty Years in the Pulpit*. New York: Bloch, 1971.

Rudin, James, and Rudin, Marcia. *Prison or Paradise: The New Religious Cults*. Philadelphia: Fortress Press, 1980.

Rusk, Tom, and Miller, Patrick D. *The Power of Ethical Persuasion.* New York: Viking Penguin, 1993.

Schreck, Alan. *Your Catholic Faith: A Question and Answer Catechism.* Ann Arbor, MI: Servant Publications, 1989.

Schuckman, Louis. Letter to Rabbi Alan Silverstein. Caldwell, NJ, September 5, 1993.

Schulweis, Harold. "The Hyphen Between the Cross and the Star." In Harold Schulweis, ed., *In God's Mirror: Reflections and Essays.* Hoboken, NJ: KTAV, 1990, pp. 168–177.

——, ed. *In God's Mirror: Reflections and Essays.* Hoboken, NJ: KTAV, 1990.

——. "Inreach: Ways Toward Family Empowerment." In Harold Schulweis, ed., *In God's Mirror: Reflections and Essays.* Hoboken, NJ: KTAV, 1990, pp. 188–198.

——. "My Zeyda, His Grandchildren, and the Synagogue." Wilstein Institute, *Comment and Analysis*, p. 1.

——. "Peering into the Limbo of Judeo-Christian Beliefs." In Carol Diamant, ed., *Jewish Marital Status.* Northvale, NJ: Jason Aronson, 1989, pp. 238–245.

Sequoia, Anna. *The Official J.A.P. Handbook.* New York: New American Library, 1982.

Singer, Suzanne. "A 'Critical Mass' of Judaism May Prevent Intermarriage." *Moment* 16:5 (October 1991): 4.

Sklare, Marshall. "American Jewry—The Ever-Dying People." *Midstream* 22:6 (June–July 1976): 17–27.

Strassfeld, Sharon, and Green, Kathy, eds. *The Jewish Family Book.* New York: Bantam Books, 1981.

Ticktin, Max. "The Blessings of Being a Grandfather." In Sharon Strassfeld and Kathy Green, eds., *The Jewish Family Book.* New York: Bantam Books, 1981.

Twerski, Abraham. "Animals and Angels: Spirituality in Recovery." Aliquippa, PA: Gateway Rehabilitation Center, 1990, videotape.

Waldoks, Moshe. *The Big American Book of Jewish Humor.* New York: Harper & Row, 1981.

Warren, Andrea, and Wiedenkeller, Jay. *Everybody's Doing It: How to Survive Your Teenager's Sex Life (And Help Them Survive It Too).* New York: Viking Penguin, 1993.

Wasser, Joel. *We Are Family*. New York: United Synagogue Youth, 1993.

Winer, Mark. "Mom, We're Just Dating." In Carol Diamant, ed., *Jewish Marital Status*. Northvale, NJ: Jason Aronson, 1989, pp. 228–230.

Winer, Mark, and Meir, Aryeh. *Questions Jewish Parents Ask about Intermarriage: A Guide for Jewish Families*. New York: American Jewish Committee, 1993.

Wolfson, Ron. *The Art of Jewish Living: Hanukkah*. New York: Federation of Jewish Men's Clubs, 1990.

——. *Jewish Family Education*. Los Angeles: University of Judaism Series, 1990, pamphlet.

Wolpe, David J. *Explaining God to Children: A Jewish Perspective*. New York: Henry Holt, 1993.

Woocher, Jonathan. "Jewish Survival Tactics." *Hadassah Magazine* 74:10 (June–July 1993): 10–13.

Yankelovich, Daniel. *New Rules: Searching for Self-Fulfillment in a World Turned Upside Down*. New York: Random House, 1981.

Index

Abramawitz, Yosef, 146
Akiba, 155
Allen, Woody, 87
Anker, Charlotte, 15
Anti-Semitism
    nonobservant Jews and, 55
    religious relativism and, 35–38
    stereotyping, parent/young-
        adult dialogues, 88
Assimilation
    American culture and, 34–35,
        58–60
    intermarriage and, 11, 44
    nonobservant Jews and, 56
    segregation contrasted,
        childrearing guidelines,
        102–104
Attarian, John, 82

Baptism, *bris* contrasted, 168–169
Bar/bat mitzvah, confirmation
    contrasted, 169–171
Baron, Salo, 154
Bellah, Robert, 130
Berger, Peter, 129
Biblical injunctions, against
    intermarriage, Jewish
    education, 5–6

Bloom, Harold, 58
Brandeis, Louis D., 159
Brauner, Ronald, 175
Bris, baptism contrasted,
    168–169
Buber, Martin, 152
Burstein, Chaya, 185

Camp Ramah, 199
Camps
    Camp Ramah, 199
    high-school-age children,
        63–65
    intermarriage opposition
        program and, xix
Charity, Jewish identity and,
    141–148
Childrearing
    conversion and, 9
    dual religious training
        child's choice, 15–17
        conflicts within, 12–14
    Jewish identity and, 3–4, 9–11,
        50
    religious identity and, 11–12
    secularism and, 11–12
Childrearing guidelines, 99–125.
    See also Parental guidelines;

Childrearing (*continued*)
  Parent/young-adult
    dialogues
  December dilemma and,
    104–106
  ethics and, 110–112
  hands-on activities and,
    113–114
  identity formation and,
    118–121
  intermarriage and, 106–108
  Jewish education
    family education, 123–125
    formal, 121–123
    informal, 114–118, 123
  Jewish heritage and, 109–110
  Jewish identity and, 100
  overview of, 99–100
  parental role models, 100–102
  segregation of children,
    102–104
Christianity
  childrearing, dual religious
    training, 12–17
  intermarriage and, 38–40
  Judaism contrasted, 167–177
    bar/bat mitzvah/
      confirmation, 169–171
    *bris/*baptism, 168–169
    death, 171–172
    Hanukkah/Christmas,
      173–175
    Passover/Easter, 176–177
    synagogue/church, 172–173
  Messianic Judaism and, 21–24
  mixed marriages and, 19–20
  religia concept and, 91

  religious relativism and, 35–38
Christmas. *See* December
  dilemma
Circumcision, baptism
  contrasted, 168–169
Coles, Robert, 180
College-age children
  grandparent guidelines,
    financial assistance, 189
  parental guidelines, 65–66
  resources for, 202–203
College-age youth,
  intermarriage opposition
  program and, xix
Community
  Jewish identity and, 138,
    141–148
  parental responsibility and,
    91–93
Community solutions, mixed
  marriages, 33–34
Confirmation, *bar/bat mitzvah*
  contrasted, 169–171
Conservative movement
  Jewish identity and, 131,
    146–147
  Jewish marriage and,
    xvii–xviii
Conversion
  intermarriage and, 8–9, 50
  net Jewish losses to, xvii, 8–9
  rabbinic involvement and,
    44–46
Council of Jewish Federations
  (CJF), xvii, 4
Courtship. *See* Dating
Cowan, Paul, 17, 18, 85, 87, 88, 158

Cowan, Rachel, 17, 18, 85, 87, 88
Culture
    childrearing guidelines,
        99–100
    Christian hegemony, 38–40
    gentile friendships, parent/
        young-adult dialogues and,
        80
    Jewish survival and, 4
    mixed marriages and, 19–20,
        34–35
    parental guidelines and, 58–60
    religious identity and, 11–12
Custody battles, mixed
    marriages and, 17–18

Danan, Julie Hilton, 182
Dating
    childrearing guidelines and,
        108
    intermarriage opposition
        program and, xix
    parental guidelines, 66–67
    parent/young-adult
        dialogues, 71–95. *See also*
        Parent/young-adult
        dialogues
Day schools
    intermarriage opposition
        program and, xviii
    Solomon Schechter day
        schools, 199
Death, Judaism/Christianity
    contrasted, 171–172
December dilemma
    childrearing guidelines and,
        104–106

gentile friendships, parent/
    young-adult dialogues and,
    79–80
grandparent guidelines, 183
Hanukkah/Christmas,
    Christianity/Judaism
    contrasted, 173–175
Dershowitz, Alan, 145–146
Dietary laws, Jewish heritage,
    childrearing guidelines
    and, 109–110
Divorce, mixed marriages and,
    17–18, 20
Donin, Hayim Halevy, 64, 65,
    113

Easter, Passover contrasted,
    176–177
Eisen, Arnold, 4, 55–56
Ethical Culture. *See* Secular
    humanism
Ethics
    childrearing guidelines and,
        110–112
    Jewish heritage, childrearing
        guidelines and, 109–110
Extended family
    parental guidelines and, 61–62
    parent/young-adult dialogues
        and, 93–95

Faith community, mixed
    marriages, 33–34
Family education, childrearing
    guidelines, 123–125
Family focus, intermarriage
    opposition program and,
    xviii

Fay, Martha, 59, 186
Fields, Harvey J., 6
Film. *See* Media
Financial assistance,
    grandparent guidelines,
    187–190
Fisch, Aharoni, 22
Fishman, Sylvia Barack, 121
Fitzpatrick, Jean Grasso, 135–136
Fuchs, Steven, 34
Futility argument, parental
    guidelines, 50–53

Gentile friendships
    parent guidelines and, 58–60
    parent/young-adult dialogues
    and, 77–80
Gillman, Neil, 140
Gittelsohn, Roland B., 74, 75
Goldman, Ari, 139
Goldstein, Alice, 121
Goodman-Malamuth, Leslie, 14
Gordis, Daniel, 147
Gordis, Robert, xvi, 147
Gordon, Albert, 35, 39
Gore, Albert, Jr., 132
Grandparent guidelines,
    179–190
    financial assistance, 187–190
    Jewish identity, 186–187
    nonobservant Jews, 180–181
    overview of, 179–180
    parent resistance and, 184–186
    ritual, power of, 181–184
Green, Kathy, 118
Greenberg, Sidney, 148
Griffith, Melanie, 84
Grishaver, Joel, 105, 184

Hands-on activities,
    childrearing guidelines
    and, 113–114
Hertzberg, Arthur, 163
Heschel, Abraham Joshua, 134,
    138–139
High-school-age children,
    parental guidelines, 63–65
Holidays
    childrearing guidelines and,
    104–106
    gentile friendships, parent/
    young-adult dialogues and,
    79–80
    grandparent guidelines,
    power of, 181–184
    Hanukkah/Christmas,
    Christianity/Judaism
    contrasted, 173–175
    Jewish identity and, 134, 138,
    143
    mixed marriages and, 19–20
    Passover/Easter, Christianity/
    Judaism contrasted, 176–177
Holocaust
    gentile friendships, parent/
    young-adult dialogues and,
    78–79
    Jewish identity and, 147
Hubbard, L. Ron, 27
Hypocrisy, extended family
    parental guidelines and, 61–62
    parent/young-adult dialogues
    and, 93–95

Identity formation, childrearing
    guidelines and, 118–121

Informal education
  childrearing guidelines and,
    informal, 114–118, 123
  high-school-age children,
    63–65
  intermarriage opposition
    program and, xix
Intellectualism, Jewish identity
  and, 148–159
Intermarriage. *See also* Mixed
  marriages
  biblical injunctions against, 5–6
  childrearing guidelines and,
    106–108
  Christian attitude toward,
    38–40
  conversion and, 8–9
  dating/marriage criteria
    compared, parent/young-
    adult dialogues, 75–77
  intermarriage opposition
    program to, xviii–xx
  Jewish survival and, 49–50
  patriarchs and, 7–8
  rabbinic participation in,
    45–46
  rate of, xvii, xviii, xx, 3, 42–44
Israel
  identity formation,
    childrearing guidelines
    and, 120
  nonobservant Jews and, 55
Israel, Richard, 75, 90
Israel experience
  financial assistance,
    grandparent guidelines,
    188–189

high-school-age children, 65
intermarriage opposition
  program and, xix
resources for, 201–202

Jewish education
  adult, 203–204
  biblical injunctions against
    intermarriage and, 5–6
  childrearing guidelines
    family education, 123–125
    formal, 121–123
    informal, 114–118, 123
  college-age children, 65–66
  early childhood, 197
  financial assistance,
    grandparent guidelines, 188
  high-school-age children,
    63–65
  intermarriage opposition
    program and, xviii, xix, xx
  Solomon Schechter day
    schools, 199
  synagogue schools, 197–198
Jewish heritage
  childrearing guidelines and,
    109–110
  identity formation,
    childrearing guidelines
    and, 118–121
  parental guidelines and, 62
Jewish identity, 129–159
  childrearing and, 3–4, 9–12,
    50, 100
  grandparent guidelines,
    186–187

Jewish education (*contined*)
  hands-on activities and,
    childrearing guidelines,
    113–114
  high-school-age children,
    63–65
  intellectualism and, 148–159
  mixed marriages and, 20–21,
    40–42
  nonobservant Jews and, 54–58
  parental responsibility and,
    91–93
  pluralism and, 129–130
  secular humanism and, 30–33
  self-fulfillment through,
    130–132
  social activism and, 141–148
  spirituality and ritual, 132–141
Jewish survival
  culture and, 4
  future prospects for, 163–166
  intermarriage and, xvii, 9–11,
    46, 49–50
  nonobservant Jews and, 55
  parental responsibility, 91
Johnson, Catherine, 76–77

Kaplan, Mordecai, 91
Kaye, Deborah, 183
Kennedy, Ruby Jo, 44
Koch, Edward I., 146
Kornhaber, Arthur, 180
Kosmin, Barry A., 63
Kroloff, Charles, 74
Kushner, Harold, 32, 132, 133,
  138, 157

Lamdan, Elimelech, 25, 26

Lebeau, William H., 203
Levey, Larry, 23
Levin, Sunie, 184–185, 186
Lewis, Shari, 185
Lipstadt, Deborah, 34
Lumet, Sidney, 84

Maimonides, 140, 149
Marder, Janet, 61
Margolis, Robin, 14
Marital quality, mixed
  marriages, 17–20
Maslow, A. A., 131
Mayer, Egon, xvii, 9
McCollister, John C., 168, 174,
  176
McGoldrick, Monica, 85
Media
  childrearing guidelines and,
    108
  parent/young-adult
    dialogues, 82–84
Medved, Michael, 82
Meir, Aryeh, 53, 90–91
Melting pot doctrine, culture
  and, 34–35
Messianic Judaism, mixed
  marriage and, 21–24
Miller, Patrick D., 53
Mixed marriages. *See also*
    Intermarriage
  attitudes within, xvii
  childrearing and, 9–11
  Christian attitude toward,
    38–40
  community solutions, 33–34
  culture and, 34–35

Jewish identity and, 20–21,
40–42
messianic Judaism and, 21–24
quality of, 17–20
rabbinic involvement with,
44–46
religious relativism and, 35–38
Scientology and, 27–30
secular humanism and, 30–33
transcendental meditation
and, 25–27
Unitarianism and, 24–25
Moline, Jack, 57, 100, 106–107,
108
Moline, Richard, 66

Nadich, Hadassah Ribalow, 183
Networking, available dating
partners, parent/young-
adult dialogues, 81
Non-Jews. *See* Gentile
Nonobservant Jews
grandparent guidelines,
180–181
Jewish identity and, 54–58
parental guidelines, 54–58

Ochs, Vanessa, 155
Organizations, Jewish identity
and, 141–148
Osbourne, Ronald, 16

Parental guidelines, 49–67. *See
also* Childrearing
guidelines; Parent/young-
adult dialogues
American culture and, 58–60
college-age children, 65–66

extended family and, 61–62
futility argument, 50–53
high-school-age children,
63–65
intermarriage opposition
program and, xix–xx
Jewish heritage and, 62
Jewish survival and, 49–50
nonobservant parents, 54–58
parent/child relationship,
53–54
peer relations and, 60–61
singles programs, 66–67
Parent/young-adult dialogues,
71–95. *See also* Childrearing
guidelines; Parental
guidelines
available dating partners,
80–82
dating/marriage criteria
compared, 75–77
dating stages, 72–73
extended family and, 93–95
gentile friendships and, 77–80
media influences, 82–84
overview of, 71–72
parental responsibility, 89–93
racism argument, 73–75
rejection of Jewish partners,
84–89
Paskow, Shimon, 186–187
Passover, Easter contrasted,
176–177
Patriarchs, intermarriage and,
7–8
Patrilinealism, requirements of,
10–11

Pearl, Jonathan, 83, 84
Pearl, Judith, 83, 84
Peer relations, parental
    guidelines and, 60–61
Perel, Esther, 85
Petsonk, Judy, 11, 16, 24
Pluralism
    Jewish identity and, 129–130
    parental guidelines and, 58–60
Pogrebin, Letty Cottin, 31–32,
    138
Politics, gentile friendships,
    parent/young-adult
    dialogues and, 78–79
Potok, Chaim, 153
Prager, Dennis, 19, 23, 42, 81,
    118, 122–123, 145
Prayer, Jewish identity and,
    136–137

Racism argument, parent/
    young-adult dialogues,
    73–75
Rank, Perry, 95
Reform movement, patrilineal
    proclamation of, 10, 11
Rehabilitation programs, Jewish
    identity and, 139–140
Rejection, of Jewish partners,
    parent/young-adult
    dialogues, 84–89
Relativism, religious, mixed
    marriages and, 35–38
Religia concept, Christianity
    and, 91
Religious relativism, mixed
    marriages and, 35–38
Remsen, Jim, 11, 16, 24

Reuben, Steven Carr, 12, 117
Ritual
    Jewish identity and, 132–141
    power of, grandparent
    guidelines, 181–184
Roiphe, Anne, 30, 31, 139, 145,
    158
Role models, parental,
    childrearing guidelines,
    100–102
Romano, Dugan, 76
Romanoff, Lena, 13
Romantic love, dating/marriage
    criteria compared, parent/
    young-adult dialogues,
    75–77
Rosen, Martin, 21–22
Roth, Philip, 19
Rudin, Jacob Philip, 45–46
Rudin, James, 28–30
Rudin, Marcia, 28–30
Rusk, Tom, 53, 54

Sarna, Jonathan, 163–164
Sasso, Sandy Eisenberg, 185
Scholem, Gershom, 131
Schreck, Alan, 168, 170, 174, 176
Schulweis, Harold, 37, 124, 169,
    182
Scientology, mixed marriages
    and, 27–30
Secular humanism, mixed
    marriages and, 30–33
Secularism, childrearing and,
    11–12
Segregation, of children,
    childrearing guidelines,
    102–104

Self-fulfillment, Jewish identity and, 130–132
Seltzer, Sanford, 60
Sequoia, Anna, 87
Shabbat, Jewish identity and, 138–139
Sholem, Gershom, 92
Shuckman, Louis, 52
Silverstein, Alan, 52
Singer, Suzanne, 125
Single adults, intermarriage opposition program and, xix
Singles programs
  available dating partners, parent/young-adult dialogues, 81
  parental guidelines, 66–67
Sklare, Marshall, 164
Social activism, Jewish identity, 141–148
Solomon Schechter day schools, 199
Spirituality, Jewish identity and, 132–141
Spitz, Elie, 136
Stereotyping, rejection of Jewish partners, parent/young-adult dialogues, 84–89
Strassfeld, Sharon, 118
Substance abuse, Jewish identity and, 139–140
Summer programs, intermarriage opposition program and, xix
Synagogue

childrearing guidelines and, 114–118
Christian church contrasted, 172–173
grandparent guidelines, 188
Synagogue schools, 197–198

Television. *See* Media
Telushkin, Joseph, 19, 42
Ticktin, Max, 179
Torah study, Jewish identity and, 148–149
Transcendental meditation, mixed marriages and, 25–27
12-Step programs, Jewish identity and, 139–141
Twerski, Abraham, 140

Union of American Hebrew Congregations, 12
Unitarianism, mixed marriages and, 24–25
United Synagogue Youth (USY), xix, xx

Values
  childrearing guidelines, 99–100
  gentile friendships, parent/young-adult dialogues and, 80
  Jewish heritage, childrearing guidelines and, 109–110
  Jewish identity and, 146, 151–152
  media influences, parent/young-adult dialogues, 82–84

Wagener, Oleon, 183

Waldoks, Moshe, 87

Warren, Andrea, 51

Wasser, Joel, 73

Werk, Susan, 124

Wiedenkeller, Jay, 51

Wiesel, Elie, 147

Winer, Mark L., 53, 60, 90–91

Wohlberg, Jeffrey, 159

Wolfson, Ron, 104, 106, 107, 124

Wolpe, David J., 101, 115, 116

Woocher, Jonathan, 67

Woodward, Kenneth L., 180

Yalow, Rosalyn, 155

Yammer, David, 14

Yankelovich, Daniel, 131,
    156–157

Youth groups
    high-school-age children,
        63–65
    intermarriage opposition
        program and, xix
    resources for, 200–201

About the Author

Rabbi Alan Silverstein is the International President of the Rabbinical Assembly, the association of the 1,400 rabbis affiliated with Conservative Judaism's institutions. He received his Ph.D. in Jewish history at the Jewish Theological Seminary (JTS) and is the author of *Alternatives to Assimilation: The Response of Reform Judaism to American Culture, 1840–1930*, as well as dozens of articles, booklets, and essays. For the past ten years Rabbi Silverstein has taught Conservative Judaism's approach to intermarriage, conversion, and outreach to JTS rabbinical students. He has supervised pioneering programs in serving Jewish singles, in training and involving Jews by Choice, and in seeking to bring intermarried Jews closer to Judaism. He has lectured throughout North America on topics related to Jewish continuity. Rabbi of Congregation Agudath Israel in Caldwell, New Jersey, he resides in West Caldwell, with his wife, Rita, and their children, David and Rebecca.